BEHIND THE SCENES AT
WHO WANTS TO BE A MILLIONAIRE?

BEHIND THE SCENES AT

MILLIONAIRE

TOM McGREGOR

BOXTREE

First published 1999 by Boxtree
an imprint of Macmillan Publishers Ltd
25 Eccleston Place London SW1W 9NF
and Basingstoke

Associated companies throughout the world

ISBN 0 7522 1797 6

A CIP catalogue record for this book is available from the British Library.

Designed by Blackjacks
Printed by Bathpress Colourbooks, Glasgow

PICTURE ACKNOWLEDGEMENTS
Front cover: (clockwise from top right) Mike Vaughan, Mike Vaughan,
Sven Arnstein, Brian Ritchie, Brian Ritchie, Mike Vaughan.
Back cover: Brian Ritchie (top), Sven Arnstein (bottom left).
Sven Arnstein: 9, 38, 44, 49.
Brian Ritchie: 2, 6, 8, 13, 14, 15, 16, 24, 26-7, 28, 29, 30, 31, 32-3, 34, 35,
37, 40, 42-3, 46, 47, 50, 52, 53, 54, 56, 57, 59, 60, 61, 62, 63, 64, 66, 67,
68-9, 71, 72, 74, 75, 76, 77, 78, 80, 81, 82, 83, 84, 85, 86, 87, 88, 89, 90-1,
92, 94-5, 96, 97, 98, 100, 101, 102, 114, 117, 118, 120, 121, 122, 123.
Mike Vaughan: 10, 17, 18, 20, 21, 22, 23, 48, 110, 112.
Adrian Woolfe: 12, 36, 58, 88.

CONTENTS

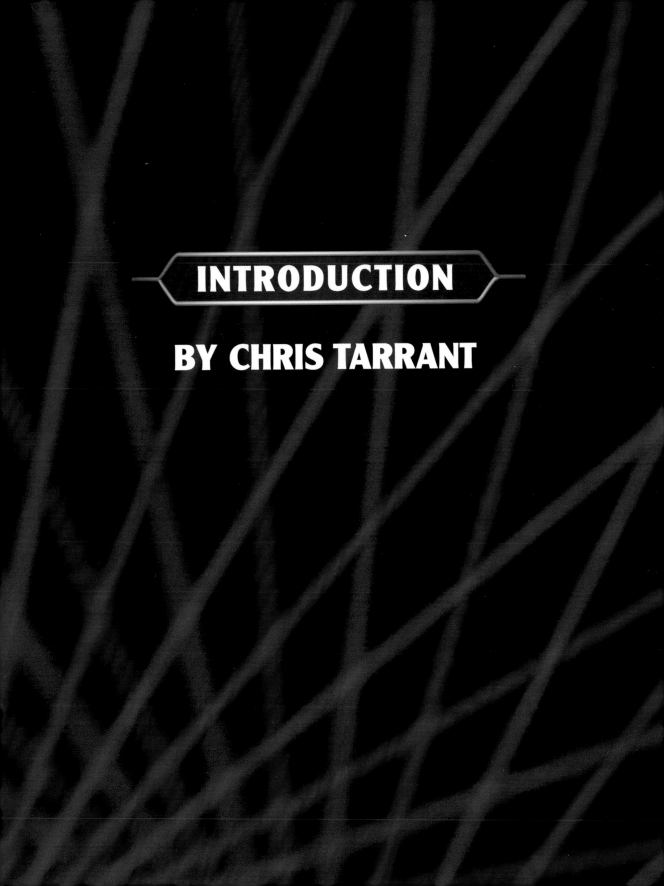

INTRODUCTION

BY CHRIS TARRANT

O ver the years I must have given away well over £1,000,000 in prize money to all sorts of people from all sorts of places on all sorts of shows, both on radio and on television.

But, and I feel a bit ashamed to admit this, I find it really hard to picture a single contestant in detail. For all of us, if we're honest, quiz show contestants tend to come and go — the lucky ones yelling with excitement and taking away huge cheques or driving off in brand new cars, the unlucky ones going away with virtually nothing or something as forgettable as a *Blankety Blank* cheque book and pen.

If you think of all the quiz shows you've watched in your life, truthfully how many of the contestants — even the big winners — do you actually remember? Probably very few; very few, that is, until *Who Wants To Be A Millionaire?*

One of the many quirky things about this show is that for one or two nights the lives of each of the contestants becomes an open book. Their hopes and dreams, their mannerisms and their reactions under extreme pressure somehow get into the very soul of all of us watching. You probably don't remember a single contestant on twenty years of *Family Fortunes* or *Countdown* and yet in just a matter of months, the winners and even the losers on *Who Wants To Be A Millionaire?* have become etched into many of our memories forever.

Who can forget big John McKeown, the bald Glasgow sewage delivery worker (and what a job that sounds!) — who had the entire nation on the edge of their seats for two nights and eventually won £64,000. Or lovely Samantha from Bradford who simply didn't know where the drink *Retsina* came from. Half the nation that night were yelling the word 'Greece' at their televisions!

And no one could ever forget Fiona from Canvey Island, who when I told her that she'd won the Fastest Finger First round and was next to play for a possible million quid, uttered the unforgettable words, 'Oh God Chris, I've wet meself!' She was an absolutely magical contestant, putting herself and the huge audience for both those nights through every conceivable agony and emotion before finally leaving

Fiona Wheeler. 'I do scream a lot. I can't help it. People think I've been let out for the day.'

us ecstatically with £32,000. For Fiona it was clearly life-changing money, and I've never been happier to write someone out a very large cheque in my life. If only it had been even more.

And then of course there was Mark Mills, the pilot from Kent, who got to within four questions of being the first person ever to win £1,000,000 on a quiz show with two lifelines left. I thought, the camera crew thought, everyone biting their nails in the control room thought, and I'm sure everyone in Britain thought that he was going to be the first person ever to win £1,000,000 on a television quiz show. Sadly, he answered the £125,000 question incorrectly and the chance was lost, but he was a very cool customer and could, and should have won the lot.

These were just a few of the unforgettable characters from the first three series. There will be many, many more because it's they who make *Who Wants To Be A Millionaire?* the huge success that it has become. A lot of people who are not normally quiz show viewers find it absolutely compulsive, but then it's not really a quiz show, it's a soap opera!

Of course, the money is relevant and the money is potentially huge, but it's the players themselves who capture the imagination, because these are real people playing for real sums of money. The very fact that *Who Wants To Be A Millionaire?* has to be open to virtually everyone means that the most unlikely people get on TV, in front of some of the biggest audiences of all time. The show is all about their raw emotions.

There's something very simple about the show and perhaps that's another reason why it works – the rules really couldn't be simpler. Once in the hotseat, if you answer fifteen questions right you win £1,000,000 – you can take your money at any time you like and, unlike any other show in the world, you actually get to see the answers before you decide whether or not to play the question.

And it has something else, David Briggs – for many years my producer at Capital Radio, who then went on to co-devise *Who Wants To Be A Millionaire?* – calls it 'shoutability'. It has tremendous shoutability. It has people all over the country on the edge of their seats shouting the answers at their TV screens. It's a great family occasion – a chance for Dad to show off, Mum to scream her disagreement and the kids to be amazed at how super-intelligent their parents really are, or more likely, how much brighter they are than their mum and dad. Above all, it's a chance for all of them to shout at the tops of their voices at the drama enfolding in front of them on their TV screen. If this is what's happening in your household, don't be embarrassed, don't be shy, you are not alone, it happens night after night in millions of homes all over the UK.

Initially of course, before we even went on air, we were criticized. A lot of people thought a prize of £1,000,000 was just too much money. Paul Smith, the executive producer, and I were asked by several journalists whether there would be counselling on hand and therapists to deal with the problems that winning £1,000,000 would bring into people's lives. Counselling would be available, of course, but I always found it an absurd question – if

John, the Glaswegian slaphead, had won £1,000,000 that night, I don't think his first thought would have been, 'Where's my analyst?' It would have been, 'Where's the bar?!'

In any case, it's important to keep this whole money thing in context. No one has yet won £1,000,000, and I keep being asked if anyone ever will. I am confident that it will happen one day – perhaps quite soon, perhaps even by the time that you are reading this!

In the meantime, it should never be forgotten that £4,000, £8,000 or £16,000 are still very large sums of money and have made a lot of people a lot happier. This money has paid off mortgages, replaced ailing vehicles and given several of our contestants the lovely feeling of being out of debt for the first time in years.

Three or four different contestants now have said to me, 'I just want to be that person' – the first person ever on a television quiz show to win £1,000,000, and that's their motivation more than the money, more than anything. It will be rather more than fifteen minutes of fame. They will be all over the papers, magazines, television and newsreels around the world. And of course, when it does happen, when we've all calmed down, we'll just start all over again with a brand new contestant trying to win another £1,000,000.

For everybody involved in the show, the crew, the audience, all of us, it will be an amazing night. The atmosphere will go through the roof and for me, personally, never mind my career, just for me as a bloke, it will be one of the most incredible nights of my life. It'll probably be me who needs the therapist – but I'm looking forward to it hugely!

Chris Tarrant, May 1999

ONE

A SHOW IN A MILLION:

HOW IT ALL BEGAN

The statistics are staggering. Over ten million phone calls from would-be contestants; up to nineteen million viewers per night; prize money that has made TV history (a total of £1,944,000 has been given away so far); foreign licensing of the programme to sixteen countries to date (including, – unusually for a British quiz show, the United States); press coverage that, for the first three series, stands several feet high and a phrase – 'Can I Phone A Friend?' – that has become a catch-phrase. Those are just some of the reasons why *Who Wants To Be A Millionaire?* has catapulted into the record books and become a global phenomenon.

And it's all such a simple idea: once in the hot-seat Chris Tarrant asks you fifteen multiple choice questions and if you answer them all correctly you walk away with £1,000,000.

So why hadn't it been done before?

Well ... imagine a different scenario. A show with no celebrity guests. No new novelty stunts. No outside broadcasts. A programme that could ruin its creators and cost ITV millions. A quiz show that wouldn't work unless the whole country knew about it. A telephone income which was at precisely zero pounds ten days before the show went on air. Contestants who haven't even been seen by the show's producers until they arrive at the studio. And, to cap it all, an unprecedented decision to transmit the show

Originating director (right) Martin Scott and Guy Freeman (left), originating producer of the first series, clutching their BAFTA Awards (for Best Light Entertainment Series 1999).

on successive nights on prime-time television. Each and every one of those ingredients is in the book of recipes for disaster. Paul Smith, the managing director of Celador (the production company which makes *Millionaire*), freely acknowledges that 'it was an enormous risk. A *huge* risk.' Chris Tarrant is characteristically more blunt: 'It's very easy to sit back now and say "Oh yeah ... *Millionaire*", but it could have been: "You know that pile of rubbish that was on last night? Well, it's on again tonight. And tomorrow!" It could have failed spectacularly and ruined everyone involved.'

The fact that it didn't – that it succeeded beyond anyone's wildest dreams – is due to an intense, complex collaborative process that lasted three years and involved a new boss at ITV, a change of

title, people who were prepared to risk their house and home, a total overhaul of the programme days before transmission and a revolution in the quiz show format.

The concept of *Who Wants To Be A Millionaire?* was brought to Celador by David Briggs, now associate producer. He had a 'vague idea' which he scribbled down on a scrap of paper and then went out to lunch a lot with Steve Knight and Mike Whitehill, now programme associates. All three men work at Celador and used to work together on London's Capital Radio and spend their lives variously writing and devising quiz shows, sketches and sitcoms (Steve and Mike worked on Jasper Carrott's *The Detectives*). Given that the idea they began to develop had similarities to a pub quiz, it was fitting that they nursed it to fruition over lunch. 'It was white-wine based,' laughs Mike. 'It could have been called *Who Wants Another Glass of Chardonnay?*'. Given that the title they originally came up with was *Cash Mountain* (a title that remained almost to transmission), *Chardonnay* might have been better ...

Jokes apart, they felt they were on to something big. Yet the problems facing Celador were also sizeable – how exactly would they raise the enormous sums of prize money, how were they going to make people keep playing the game, and why would an audience want to watch people they knew nothing about trying to win vast sums of money? At that point 'confessional' shows – the *Jerry Springer*s and *Vanessa*s of this world – were at their peak. Audiences were used to egging people on to further excesses of behaviour – not to winning a million by sitting in a chair and answering questions. What sort of enjoyment was the audience going to get in seeing other people getting rich?

The answer lies in the concept of 'shoutability'. As the idea progressed and more people got involved, it became evident that people at home would scream the answers out as hesitant contestants began to sweat. What is now one of the show's catchphrases – 'It's only easy if you know the answer' – is one of the reasons for its staggering popularity: some answers are blindingly obvious to some people, completely unknown to others. Chris Tarrant has a perfect illustration of this. 'On one of the very first nights we had this really nice, very intelligent bloke who absolutely *hated* football. He'd switch the TV off whenever he heard the word. And his fifth question, for £1,000 was, of course, about football: "Which team won the Premiership title in 1998?" Practically the whole country knew the answer was Arsenal but he had to Phone A Friend to find out. Everyone who'd been watching was *screaming* the answer at their TVs ... it's that wonderful word – "shoutability".'

But, by January 1996, they were a long way from that wonderful word. The concept had become a proper format for a show – ready for pitching to ITV. Devising the show was one thing: selling it was another. Independent television companies like

Celador can only make programmes; they can't transmit them. Only a broadcaster (in this case, ITV) can do that and they must pay for the privilege of doing so. Therefore Paul Smith had to persuade them that the idea was worth buying. As managing director of Celador, his input into the show had been enormous: 'I pitched it to Claudia Rosencrantz, controller of entertainment at the ITV network. She liked everything about it except the name (it was still called *Cash Mountain* at that time). Unfortunately, her boss didn't like anything about it – and nothing happened.' But Claudia Rosencrantz stuck with it and, with the arrival of a new boss – David Liddiment – in late 1997,

Paul Smith – he risked everything to get Millionaire *on the air.*

the idea resurfaced. The name David Liddiment may not mean much to the layman – but his achievements will. If nothing else, he'll be remembered as the man who boosted ITV's ratings by bringing *Who Wants To Be A Millionaire?* to the small screen.

But nothing is that simple and, as Paul Smith says, 'ITV's greatest concern was that we might end up giving away £1,000,000 every night.' (A wonderful way to boost the ratings and a sure-fire way to damage the network.) Trying to insure against that (they were quoted a premium of £640,000 for the

first series) was a financial impossibility. In the end, and this was the most enormous risk of all, they went into the first series without insurance. Paul Smith looks back with a wry smile now, but it certainly wasn't funny at the time. 'We knew the extreme unlikelihood of having to give away £1,000,000 every night, but David wouldn't be persuaded. I said, "Let me put you in the most extreme scenario: you're at half a million, you've got no lifelines left and if you get the next question wrong you're going to lose £468,000. Unless you're *absolutely* sure of the answer you're

going to stick at half a million. You cannot afford to have any doubt.'"

But David Liddiment had doubts.

In a last-ditch attempt to persuade him, Paul Smith went to the network headquarters, sat down with David Liddiment and Claudia Rosencrantz and asked the former if he had £250 in his wallet. 'This man is the director of programmes at ITV ... you just don't *do* that sort of thing!' he laughs. However, he did precisely that – and discovered that David Liddiment only had £230 on him. 'So I asked him to hand that over to me along with an I.O.U. for £20. Those represented his 'winnings' on an imaginary *Millionaire* so far. Then we began to play the game for real.'

If David Liddiment was more than a little surprised at being ambushed in such a peculiar way, he recovered quickly: he 'Phoned A Friend' (or rather asked Claudia Rosencrantz) on the very first question. 'I didn't expect him to do that,' says Paul Smith. 'I forgot to tell him that he was supposed to have used up all his lifelines already...' But one question later and the point was made: David Liddiment didn't know

the answer and bowed out with £500 – which he gave to charity. 'We really were playing the game for real,' remembers Paul Smith. 'I had envelopes stuffed with money: £500, £1,000, £2,000...' David Liddiment left the meeting totally convinced that the quiz would work. He recalls, 'It was only then I really began to understand the balance of the internal debate that goes on – whether to rely on your knowledge as inhibited by the amount of money you have won and could lose if you answer incorrectly. There's a fascinating complex drama taking place and I had to experience that conflict,' he says.

Perhaps that's why he did something that has never been done before: he 'stripped' the show, and ran it on successive nights instead of, as originally conceived, on a weekly basis. 'That,' says Paul Smith, 'was a masterstroke and a major contributor to the show's success.'

Yet, just days before the show was due to be aired it looked as if it was going to be an abject failure...

The first pilot

'It looked like *Seaside Special* [entertainment show in the Seventies] circa 1976. In spending so much time on the infrastructure, I'd taken my eye off the refinement of the TV structure,' says Paul Smith.

Anyone who has seen the first pilot (and not many people have, or will, it's gone to that great quiz show graveyard) would recognize the above remark as an exaggeration. The questions were there, Chris Tarrant was there, the set was there – the same basic components as you see now were there...but it just didn't *work*. The lighting was too bright; the music was wrong; there was too much chat; there was hardly any atmosphere – and the first question was for one pound. No one is going to sit on the edge of their seat wondering if someone's going to win a pound – they're going to go and make a cup of tea.

All in all, a major problem: the pilot was recorded on 12 August 1998 – with just over three weeks to go before transmission. Claudia Rosencrantz has said,

'I know they wished I hadn't seen it. The basic grammar of the show worked – but it just didn't look right.' Afterwards, Paul Smith received a letter from David Liddiment which read: 'There's no doubt that somewhere in there are glimmers of the show we all believed in... I'm confident you'll get there.' As Paul Smith says, 'What I expect he meant was: "It's a complete mess. Get it sorted or you'll never work for ITV again".'

'The period from the first pilot to transmission,' he continues, 'was terrifying. I'm not exaggerating ... I was ill with fear. The pilot had shown that the concept hadn't been fully realized. We had two weeks to turn it around and most people were saying that it

A peek into the lion's den. The Millionaire *set is one of the most sophisticated and expensive in British TV history.*

couldn't be done in time. Even worse, when the lines opened ten days before transmission we were way, way below our projected target. It looked like we were heading for a £400,000 deficit ... I didn't sleep at all – and I'm not joking when I say I told my wife and kids that the house might have to go.' Nor was he joking when he told Celador's shareholders that *Millionaire* was either going to be their *Heaven's Gate* or their *Titanic*.

So they changed it. New music was written (in a matter of days); the lighting was changed; the set was repainted and modified; the £1 became £100; a lot of the chat went – and the end result was, effectively, a totally different programme. 'The most significant change,' reflects Paul Smith, 'was the music. *That's* when we realized it was going to work. It was *so* atmospheric.' As the pilot is not available for public consumption, the closest you can get to seeing what it was like – and what an astonishing difference the new music makes – is to watch the programme with the sound turned down.

But Paul Smith was still ill. 'Apart from all the other problems, we had no idea how far the contestants would go. There are absolutely no conventional controls over the show – we didn't even know who the

contestants would be. We knew they would feel anxiety and concern, we knew we would see people go through this stress situation ... this very *comfortable* stress situation as, let's face it, there's little downside ... but we still didn't really know how they would react.'

But that all changed on the second show, with a girl called Rachel Mendez-da-Costa. Anyone who saw her will remember her shaking with nerves, unable even to hold a glass of water, providing the most riveting piece of drama that no actress, however well-rehearsed, could begin to equal. The particular brand of nail-biting tension she generated was – and remains – all her own. But one of the most extraordinary aspects of her stint in the hot-seat was the atmosphere surrounding her: the way everyone was silently willing her to win. 'I was sitting in the computer room,' says Paul Smith, 'and all of us there were just *transfixed* by this girl. It was the most extraordinary drama. When we saw Rachel we thought: "That's it ...we've really done it."'

TWO

THE WINNERS:
RACHEL MENDEZ-DA-COSTA

'I wouldn't have noticed if the audience had left and they'd brought in dancing elephants instead ...' Rachel laughs now but, months earlier, she transfixed viewers with her appearance on *Millionaire*. It was a performance that provided the programme with many firsts: she was on the first programme, she was the first female contestant; the first rollover contestant and, far more memorably, the first contestant who brought nail-biting tension and pure unadulterated edge-of-your-seat drama to the programme. On her first night she reached £500 – on the second she was a bag of nerves. And that was the night when she wouldn't have noticed the dancing elephants.

'It was *awful* on the second day' remembers the physiotherapist from Edgware. 'I was so nervous I was ill. Chris Tarrant had to physically pull me into the studio because I was clinging to the banister saying "I can't do it!".' She laughs again, adding that 'Chris Tarrant was brilliant at calming me down. I really didn't want to come back on. Then he said, "So you'll be going home with £500, then?" Well, when he put it like that...'

Four questions later, Rachel left the show with £8,000 – not a huge amount of money in *Millionaire* terms. But it wasn't the money that kept everyone riveted: it was Rachel. 'You couldn't have trained *any* actress to do that,' said Paul Smith. 'It was the best drama on TV.'

Which English county has a border with only one other?

- A: Devon
- B: Norfolk
- C: Cornwall
- D: Kent

Chris Tarrant, too, was moved by her. You could tell at the time. After she had won £4,000 – and gone through more emotions than anyone would have thought possible – he turned to the trembling girl opposite him and joked: 'What're you *like*? Will you not *do* that?' But he wasn't really joking: he himself was stressed, impressed, relieved – and he was trying to calm her down. He told her to have a drink of water. Rachel was shaking so much that she had to use both hands, and still nearly dropped her glass.

'I feel sick.'

Then came the question that stumped her – and her father. He was her Phone A Friend – and he didn't know the answer. The clock ticked; the ominous 'heart-beat' music pulsated in the background, and Rachel's voice broke. 'Dad! Help me!' she pleaded – but her father was forced to say he didn't know the answer. For anyone watching, it was one of the most riveting, compelling – and awful – moments on television. Rachel chose not to answer and left with £8,000.

Months later, and in something of an understatement, Rachel says 'We're quite an emotional family. Dad was in a real state and I felt sick and started to cry when Chris Tarrant told me that, after I'd taken the money, my guess of Cornwall would have been right, but it *was* only a guess. It was days before it clicked with me that it had to be Cornwall.

And it took me a good couple of hours to get over the fact that I hadn't won £16,000 and to start thinking "brilliant! I've got £8,000." I felt so run down at the end of it I didn't eat for two days and I felt I'd gone through a wall. I was so nervous, I'd gone as far as I physically could without fainting or actually being sick on television.' Then she giggles as she remembers something else: 'My grandma told me off because I'd sworn at Chris Tarrant – and he was so nice.'

'I still think about it. I sometimes wake up in the middle of night thinking "Oh God!"' Asked if she would do it again, Rachel shakes her head. 'No. No, I wouldn't. Too stressful ... my legs gave way when I got off stage. Also,' she adds, 'I think you get one chance in these things and I had mine. My other half would do it, though.'

Rachel's other half is Adam, and from the outset he was very much involved in Rachel's bid to be a millionaire. 'We'd just come home from our engagement party and were opening all our presents when we saw the trailer for the show,' explains Rachel. 'Adam said "go on, phone, them." I wanted *him* to try...'

'We worked out how much we needed to clear all our debts and to put a nice deposit on a house. That's not from extravagance, just debts from my college loan, the car and starting up Adam's business.'

It's worth remembering that neither Rachel nor Adam knew anything about the show when Rachel phoned in. Nor did anyone else – her bid was for the very first show in the first series. 'We were basically guinea pigs,' she remembers. 'All that we and the other contestants knew was that we'd been invited to take part in this show. We hadn't seen a preview or anything. We didn't know what to expect.'

What Rachel certainly didn't expect, after her memorable appearance, was to be invited by the *Sun,* the show's former sponsor, to live the life of a millionaire for a day. 'It was brilliant, like being a mega-star. A week after the show they came with this stretch limo, bought me an evening dress, took me to the Athenaeum in London for champagne, lunch, a spa ... it was fantastic fun. Really cool.' Then Rachel giggles again. 'When I got home all the kids in the street goggled at the limo and then asked for my autograph! And,' she finishes, 'I've been identified with *Millionaire*. At work, people *still* say "Did you see what happened on your show last night?"'

When asked if she has any regrets, Rachel looks suddenly solemn. 'Well, for a while I felt I'd had this chance to set us up for life ... and I blew it. I watch the programme sometimes but it winds me up, it's a bit like self-torture. But no ... someone gave me £8,000 for doing not very much and I'm very grateful. Everyone on the crew was so nice and I had a brilliant time. I'm glad for what I've got. It's helped a lot. It's got us onto the property ladder.'

Rachel and Adam have put her winnings into a deposit for a house. Had she won a £1,000,000 they would have married straight away but, as it is, they're sticking with their plans for a wedding in April 2000. We wish them well and hope that the big day is as memorable – for entirely different reasons – as Rachel's extraordinary appearance on *Who Wants To Be A Millionaire?*

Which English county has a border with only one other?

* A: Devon
* B: Norfolk
* C: Cornwall
* D: Kent

THREE

TELEVISIONARIES:

THE PEOPLE WHO MAKE
WHO WANTS TO BE A MILLIONAIRE?

Who Wants To Be A Millionaire? has been variously described as 'Mastermind on speed', 'The people's quiz show', 'A classy quiz show for people who don't watch quiz shows' and, by a particularly snooty broadsheet, as 'Tat with brains' (coming from them, that's a compliment.) But it does take brains – a lot of them – to make something as successful as this and there are a great many reasons why Millionaire works.

One of them is the design of the set itself. Paul Smith was never in any doubt that he wanted the contestants to be put in an environment that wasn't exactly cosy: he wanted a 'lion's den' and, thanks to set designer Andy Walmsley, that's what he got. Andy, however, immediately passes the praise on to the set-builders. 'I did the easy bit. The clever people are the ones who built the entire thing in three weeks: John Frost Scenery. They never get any credit and they should.'

Apart from being modest, Andy Walmsley is fascinating. 'I come from the classic, clichéd showbiz family. My mother was a fire-eater (clichéd?) and my dad a comedian. I'm useless as a performer. I can't sing and I'm not funny – so, for me, being a designer was the next best thing.'

It turns out he began his career at fifteen designing a set for Paul Daniels, and later earned a reputation for Fifties-based shows including Buddy, Elvis: The Musical, Only the Lonely and Happy Days. 'Ironic, really, because I wasn't born until 1966! But I've done Boogie Nights, which was set in the Seventies, and we've just opened with Electric Dreams, which is Eighties, so I'm catching up. I've had a very, very strange career,' he says with a grin. 'One minute I'm doing Broadway and the next I'm doing Blankety Blank.'

The production crew: (front row, left to right) Paul Kirrage, director; David Briggs, associate producer; Chris Tarrant; Paul Smith, executive producer; Colman Hutchinson, producer; Sarah Gregson, director of business and legal affairs. (back row, left to right) Adrian Woolfe, head of marketing and publicity; Steve Springford, director of production; Brian Pearce, lighting director; Patricia Mordecai, director; Chris Goss, computer systems designer; Mark Hopkins, finance director; Helen Wood, production manager and Andy Walmsley, set designer.

As he speaks, he wanders onto the set itself – and the floor wobbles slightly under his weight. It's something that astonishes everyone: it looks so incredibly solid on TV yet it 'gives' when you walk on it. Andy recoils in mock-horror when asked if it's cheap. 'Cheap? It's extremely expensive. It's one-inch thick perspex. Costs an absolute fortune. So do many of the other materials used. Most of the set has industrial finishes – lots of very expensive chrome. There was actually more for the pilot but we got rid of it. It looked too shiny and tacky – and if there's one thing *Millionaire* has proved, it's that quiz shows don't have to be all neon, glitzy and tacky.' He then points out various elements of the design, leaving one in no doubt that this is one very sophisticated set.

So how much did it cost?

'£100,000 more than it was supposed to.'

Paul Smith later corroborates this. 'Yes,' he says with a grin. 'That was another of our worries at the beginning. We had a budget of £50,000 for the set and we ended up spending three times that amount...' These figures may not mean much on their own, but they take on a new perspective when you realize that a figure of £18,000 is quite common for a prime-time entertainment show set.

The expense of the *Millionaire* set, it transpires, is partly because of the materials used and partly because of the inspirations behind Andy's set. It has unusual references. 'The bowl shape,' says Andy, 'was

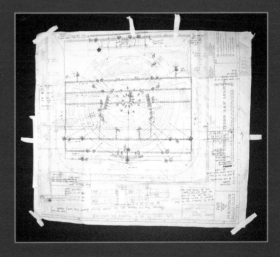

The set: inspired by sci-fi films – and the Coliseum in Rome.

Director of production Steve Springford outside
Millionaire's 'home' – the studios at Elstree.

inspired by the Riddler's lair in *Batman Forever*.' Then he laughs. 'A neat visual joke, when you think about it'. Other details were inspired by the courtroom scene in *Judge Dredd* and the incubation room in *Jurassic Park*. 'It's really unusual,' he continues, 'for a quiz show set to be based on science fiction, but the best designed films are almost always sci-fi, so it made sense.'

'The thing about this set,' he points out, 'is that it's not actually the best I've designed. It works so well because of all the other elements of the show. I think the best set I've ever designed was for *Ice Warriors*.'

What?

'Exactly. Nobody remembers it. The set cost just under £1,000,000 – that *never* happens. But the programme was one of TV's greatest ever flops. I think they lost a million viewers every week. Complete disaster.'

But there was a potential disaster connected to *Millionaire*'s set as well. Director of production, Steve Springford explains that 'The first two series were filmed at the TV studios in Wembley – TV studios that are usually hired out by the day. The problem with this show is that we need the set every night for up to three weeks at a time.'

Doesn't sound *that* problematic.

'No, but it's what we had to do with the set after those three weeks. We had to store it somewhere, and that costs £400 a week. It also meant it had to be dismantled – which means it gets knocked about and damaged – and physically moved.' For those who still think the set is small, think again. It takes twelve pantechnicons to move it ...

'So I had this idea,' says Steve, 'that if we hired a film studio – which are often hired out for months or years at a time – that could be *Millionaire*'s "home".'

Millionaire's home is a strange place. Film studios are not glamorous places: they're basically a succession of huge empty barns with little doors that you could mistake for leading to a prostitute's lair instead of the Riddler's – they have red lights outside that flash while recording is in progress... The set is plonked in the middle of one of those barns at Elstree (where the first three original *Star Wars* films were made) and there it will remain for the foreseeable future. 'We won't be using it all the time,' explains

Steve. 'In fact we won't be using it for *most* of the time, so we're looking into hiring it out.' Word is that some overseas producers are looking into using the studios as *Who Wants To Be A Millionaire?* fever spreads to other countries.

Another of the advantages of basing the show at Elstree is that there's enough room in the 'barn' for the audience VIP area. 'It's mainly for visitors to the set,' says Steve, 'but it caters for the audience over-flow as well.' This overflow has been something of a bone of contention in the media: papers have picked up on stories of people who thought they were going to be seated in the audience and found themselves in the VIP area, watching the show on a screen. 'It *is* a problem,' says Steve. 'Audience tickets for TV shows are free and, because of that, people don't turn up. It's not unusual for only sixty people to turn up for every hundred tickets given out. We've been accused of deception, but actually we're victims of our own success. People *do* tend to show up for *Millionaire*. I'm not sure what the answer is, really. We regard the audience as incredibly important. They're a vital part of the show and we want to look after them – but I don't want to have to charge them.'

Instead, he has organized free parking and tea and coffee. It might not sound like much, but it's more

Plugging in the podium. A familiar sight on set – but unseen by viewers.

than TV audiences normally get. They also, of course, get a chance of appearing in the audience of *Who Wants To Be A Millionaire?*

Another major part of *Millionaire*'s success is invisible. It's also revolutionary for a quiz show: it's the music. And it's all the more extraordinary when composer Keith Strachan says that 'we had just days to compose it.' That's because, after that famous first pilot, everyone involved with the show realized that the original music was, to put it mildly, rather unsuitable. 'It just didn't have any drama at all,' remembers Paul Smith. Part of the idea behind that original music, in fact, was that it could be made into a single to release with the show, to be recognized as the *Millionaire* theme.

But that went out the window – and in came Keith Strachan and his son Matthew. 'We've worked together before and, as this was such a mammoth job, we decided to pool our resources and do it again.'

A mammoth job? But there's not that much music; just a few notes here and there to heighten the tension and that rather nice loud burst when people get the questions right.

'No,' says Keith with a laugh. And, sure enough, if anyone can tear themselves away from the drama and concentrate on the music they'll be in for a mammoth surprise. On *Millionaire*, there are 140 music cues (that's 140 different pieces of music) and the music is played for very nearly the entire duration of the show. That's unheard of in a quiz/entertainment show.

'When Celador told us they wanted drama,' explains Keith Strachan, ' I said then you need music all the way through, and something big, bold and almost orchestral in style. Something like a John Williams score for a Spielberg movie ... *ET* or *Raiders of the Lost Ark*. Concentrating on brass and string rather than drums. The music for normal quiz shows – and I've done quite a few of them myself so I'm not being abusive – is usually very light: plinky plonky things to jolly you along.'

No one could describe the music that Keith and Matthew composed as 'plinky plonky.'

And it's amazingly intricate. It also follows an established film technique, starting in C minor, and rising in semi-tones. And each one of the 140 pieces is cued in to a precise moment of the show. There's a

piece for each question, a piece for when Chris Tarrant finds out if the answer's correct, a piece for when the answer's correct ... and so on. The only time it stops for any length of time is when the contestants get to their 'safe havens' of £1,000 and £32,000: it's a subtle mechanism to release tension. Then it starts again and the tension starts to build.

The whole music package lasts about an hour and a half. 'You have to work out how long a piece of music will be needed in the *studio*,' says Keith. 'Obviously some of it will be edited out, but there has to be enough to keep going if a contestant makes a mistake or takes ages or changes their minds. Originally, each cue lasted for thirty-two seconds. That wasn't enough. Now they last for three minutes.'

And some of it, of course, has never been heard by the audience or the contestants. The cues after someone wins £250,000 and of course £1,000,000 have yet to be transmitted. Two more progressions, each with its own tune, take the show to, in Keith's words, 'a big, bashing, Tchaikovsky-type ending. Not,' he adds with a wry smile, 'that anyone will be listening at that point. They'll all be screaming their heads off.'

Not many people know this, but audiences — or at least some of the older members of audiences — have screamed their heads off (or maybe swayed gently) to Keith's music in the past. 'Yes, I've got a No.1 hit to my name — Cliff Richard's "Mistletoe and Wine".'

Now who said anything about plinky plonky stuff?

Keith's background, in fact, is extremely varied. He has directed plays and musicals in the theatre, written songs and music for a whole host of people and programmes and, in 1980, formed the band Wall Street Crash.

One musician Keith didn't compose for is a cabaret singer called Barry Douglas. Now he never will. Barry gave up singing, reverted to his real name of Brian Pearce, became a cameraman and, later, a lighting director. He's come a long way since he buried Barry, and now he's sitting on the set of *Millionaire*, looking up at the lights that so memorably

Grams operator Barry Mizen — he's the man responsible for mixing the music.

Lighting director Brian Pearce and varilite operator Mark Ninnim in the lighting gallery.

cascade down on the audience and the contestants during moments of drama. The lights that he, as lighting director, decided to use.

'They're called varilites,' he says. 'They're commonly used for rock 'n' roll concerts but not normally for TV and certainly not for quiz shows. They were actually developed by Genesis for their live concerts.'

And they were absent in the first pilot of the show. 'To be honest, at that stage we were treating *Millionaire* as a normal quiz show, concentrating on people's faces and the breaks for commercials. It was after our famous first pilot that Paul Smith said, "Throw out the rule book and just do it. Be bolder, give it more attack, more bite. You have a completely open book".'

The varilites and the way they're used are a crucial part of *Millionaire*'s success. Ordinary lamps used in most shows are not computer-operated. Varilites are, and at the touch of a button you can control the width and intensity of the beam, zoom in and out and play with a whole range of patterns inside the lights.

As with the music, the lighting subtly changes the mood on-set – without people really being aware of it. 'They play an important part in getting the audience going,' says Brian. 'If the lights go down then so does the eye. And they help generate tension ... they remain light blue until the £1,000 question and then get progressively darker. And when we get to question ten (for £32,000) we have the big blackout. They trickle down across the audience to focus the eye on the person in the middle.'

So let's pause a minute and consider why some contestants have expressed surprise at how nervous they were on set. They're sitting smack in the middle of the Riddler's lair; they're listening to adrenalin-pumping music; they're being washed by lights that help create tension and they're sitting *below* the audience, under a spotlight. And – this probably helps as well – they're trying to win £1,000,000 ...

But will anyone ever win £1,000,000?

The team largely responsible for the format – Paul Smith, David Briggs, Steve Knight and Mike Whitehill – are themselves under a spotlight, being interrogated about their creation.

'Yes, says Paul Smith. 'All of us involved in the show want someone to win that million. It will be good for us and good for everyone. The thought of giving it away fills one with *enormous* excitement. If we don't get there ... well, the seduction process has been so exciting – indeed they say anticipation is nine-tenths of enjoyment. But I hope we get there.' Everyone echoes this statement and it doesn't ring hollow. If you think about it, giving away £1,000,000 – ('We're not going to give it away,' cautions Mike Whitehill. 'Contestants do actually work for it.') – will give the show ultimate credibility. And it's true that everyone wants that to happen. Everyone on the production team gets as carried away as the audience – in fact they're *part* of the audience – and shout at the TV monitors whilst the show is in the making. There's also an unspoken rivalry between the two directors, Paul Kirrage and Patricia Mordecai, who direct alternate shows: each wants to be the one who directs the £1,000,000 episode.

But what of the critics who say that the show is specifically designed to make people stop playing before they win a million?

'Not true,' says Paul Smith. 'I'm not saying it's going to be easy to win a million – we've already proved that and we *had* to prove it to ITV, but it's perfectly possible. People are becoming much more sophisticated in the way they use their lifelines.' Everyone agrees on this, and they embark on an animated discussion about the best use of lifelines. 'I'll give this advice,' offers Paul Smith. 'The lifeline you should use first is Ask The Audience. There's no point in using that for the hardest questions as the chances are they'll be guessing. And use Phone A Friend as late as possible.'

'Yes,' agrees Mike Whitehill, 'and I'd advise people to really think hard about which friend to call for which particular subject ... think about who might be good at science, geography or whatever. £1,000,000 will go,' he adds. 'In a pub quiz there's always someone who gets every question right. And we noticed that two of the blokes who won £125,000 didn't play their lifelines early. They held on until the money was considerable. People are beginning to play the game more cannily.'

'Remember,' says David Briggs, 'the only definitive lifeline is 50:50; it's the only lifeline that offers a certainty. It transpires that they went through 'hideously complicated' discussions about the lifelines whilst devising the programme; trying to tempt people to go for the next prize while remaining fair to them. Before arriving at the three that now exist, there were countless others contemplated and rejected. Amongst them were giving the contestant the option to change the question, having a panel of experts to hand and having a friend constantly at the other end of a phone. In retrospect, all of them seem so incredibly *wrong* – but retrospect is easy. And it shows just how, in Steve Knight's words, 'making a quiz show is difficult. It takes intelligence and skill.'

Further illustration of this is found in letting the contestant see the question before deciding to

Floor manager Griff Evans enjoying a light-hearted moment during rehearsals .

David Hogg (above) answering the £64 000-winning question. Mark Manley (below) looking pensive at £16,000.

answer it, and in giving them the 'safe havens' of £1,000 and £32,000. They seem so obvious now, but at the time they were all part of the agonized discussions about giving people a chance, about challenging people's minds against financial considerations, about how brave and bright people might be; about pitting emotion against money. There were countless other discussions as well, one of which centred on contestants who didn't make it to the hot-seat: would they get fed up and think the whole thing was a waste of time?

During the research for this book, only one dissatisfied customer has been found. He thought it was all 'stupid' and that 'I had better things to do with my time.' So, one might ask, why did he agree to come on the show, travel to London at someone else's expense, be put up for a night in a four-star hotel, be fed and watered and spend a day on the set of the most popular television show currently being aired? One can only guess that he was absolutely convinced he would win Fastest Finger First – and was thoroughly annoyed that he didn't.

And that leads to another unique aspect of *Who Wants To Be A Millionaire?* – the fact that the contestants are unknown to anyone on the show – and that they really are 'ordinary people'.

'There's usually a convention in quiz shows that, to guarantee it's an effective piece of entertainment, one has to pre-select the contestants,' says Paul Smith. 'Auditions are held and producers go around the country interviewing people to see if their legs are long enough, if their eyes are blue enough, if they've got the right sort of hair and all that sort of thing. They've somehow got to be the salt of the earth on one hand and physically attractive on the other. The fact that we can't exercise any of those controls (because people are actually paying money – via a phone call – to try to take part) was a prospect that terrified us all. It's turned out to be the show's strength – and its potential weakness. But it's made it the people's quiz show, and we've had them all...the only stipulations we make are that contestants must be sixteen or over, they mustn't have a live criminal record, and they can't be employed by any of the companies connected with the show.'

But what about...?

'We can only do so much about criminal records. Access to them is restricted by law.'

This is true. Because of this restriction, there is no completely foolproof way, during the selection process, of finding out if someone is lying about having a current criminal record. They are, however, asked at three different stages if they have one and their names are checked against a press cuttings database. They must also sign a legally binding form to verify their eligibility on that count and other rules of the competition.

Moving swiftly along ... the fact that all contestants are unknown entities has, in fact, proved to be a masterstroke. Worries that audiences wouldn't really care about the contestants because they knew nothing about them faded away. It quickly became apparent that people were riveted by the contestants and that, as Mike Whitehill says, 'the amounts of prize money were less important than we thought.' This is borne out by the fact that the two contestants who left audiences spellbound – Rachel Mendez-da-

Costa and Fiona Wheeler – won £8,000 and £32,000 respectively. 'People's aspirations to wealth are very different,' says Mike. 'Of course people who win vast amounts make headlines, but for one person £1,000 may be a lot and they'd be happy to take that.'

And, perhaps because audiences know practically nothing about the contestants, they make snap judgements about them. The studio audience certainly does: as they leave the studio there are constant refrains of 'I really wanted her to win' or 'He was a bit too big for his boots' or 'He was really nice, wasn't he?' All this about people they've never met.

And then you identify the final, magical ingredient of *Who Wants To Be A Millionaire?* An ingredient that no one could ever have invented. People.

As *Who Wants To Be A Millionaire?* continues, as contestants become more sophisticated, and as audiences and the production team will them to win a million, a question begs to be asked. Some press reports have accused Celador of pocketing vast sums of money from the phone-line and of having massive amounts sloshing about in its coffers. But just how much money is in the pot?

'I'll tell you,' says Paul Smith, opening a file. 'And, by the way, all this information is in the public domain. In the past we received around three and a half million calls per series and, at the end of the last series, we were £1,200,000 in credit. We hope to add around another million for the next series.'

So that would make just over two million available. Supposing the £125,000 barrier is broken and someone wins a million ... or two people do ... or several people win half a million?

'Well, there's obviously enough to pay the first £2,000,000. ITV has pledged to pay the next £1,000,000 – and we're now insured for a fourth million.'

So they're obviously expecting something to happen. And it just might. The prizes are creeping up. In series one they gave away £377,000, in series two it was nearly double that at £660,000. In series three the winners netted £840,500 and in series four ... well, what if they're invaded by an army from *Mastermind* and have to give away more than £4,000,000?

'Good question,' says Paul Smith with a grin. 'But that's part of the excitement, part of the suspense. What if ...?'

FOUR

THE WINNERS:
MARK MILLS

Whcontestants are getting smarter
about how they play the game, Mark
Mills is the name they tend to mention. Famously, he
reached question 12 (opposite) – for £125,000 –
with two lifelines left, chose to answer without using
them ... and got the answer wrong.

Why did he do it?

The answer lies partly in Mark's line of work: he's
a pilot. 'I'm usually incredibly cautious – I have to be!
– and I didn't feel I could trust the audience with that
question. Also, I didn't feel that the people I'd lined up
to phone would know either.' (Later, his friends corrob-
orated that: none of them did know the answer.) But
there was another reason for Mark doing what he did.
'I was so excited, I was on a roll, there were no lives at
stake ... so I thought "Oh what the hell?" I thought I'd

come there with nothing so it didn't matter if I went
away with nothing... My heart was racing but as soon
as I got in the chair I made my mind up to go for gold.'

He didn't, of course, go away with nothing. He had
secured £64,000, risked it, and ended up with half
that. But it was still enough to fulfil one of the dreams
he would have realized with £1,000,000 – to go to
Peru. The other dream – 'buying a helicopter; call it a
busman's holiday, but up till now I've only flown planes'
– has to remain a dream, but the money is enough to
get him helicopter lessons and, hopefully, a commercial licence. 'I'm really happy. £32,000 was a fantastic
present for my 34th birthday that same week.'

Paul Smith at Celador reckons that if someone
wins a million it will be by using tactics such as
Mark's. 'He went for a high level question, wasn't
quite sure about the answer but didn't use a lifeline

'Avenues and Alleyways', sung by Tony Christie, was the theme song to which Seventies TV series?

♦ A: The Pallisers   **♦ B: The Protectors**

♦ C: The Persuaders   **♦ D: The Professionals**

as he wasn't certain they would work. He was saving them for later. In the end that didn't work – but they were good tactics.'

Mark was stunned to get on the show in the first place. 'I got the call on my mobile when I was teeing-up on the golf course ... totally out of the blue. Then, when I came to the studios, I was absolutely useless in rehearsals, so I was amazed that I won Fastest Finger First – especially as I knew that the lady sitting next to me was a secretary.'

What's that got to do with anything?

Mark laughs. 'The question was about arranging four keys on a keyboard in left-to-right order ... I was really surprised she didn't get it.' She wasn't the only one: Mark's finger wasn't just the fastest – it was the only one to come up with the correct answer.

The lady sitting next to him, of course, *did* know the correct answer. But, in common with several other contestants on previous series, she forgot to do something vital. Something that you're repeatedly reminded to do in rehearsals: press the OK button once you've chosen your answer...

Given Mark's line of work, he's unlikely to forget to press the correct button. 'To me,' he says with a laugh, 'the OK and Delete buttons were the same as safety or eject. They were vital.'

The computer company directors who Mark flies around Europe will no doubt be delighted know that their pilot kept his wits about him – even under enormous stress.

'I just can't describe what the pressure is like when you're up there in front of nearly twenty million people,' says Mark. 'I'm sure my bank manager would have said to keep the £64,000 – but I decided to go for £125,000 and every time I make a decision I stick with it. Yes, I've had verbal abuse from my mates,' he says with a smile, 'but I've never been turned on by money ... more by adrenalin. And that night was the most fun I've ever had in an adrenalin junkie sort of way.' It was fun for Chris Tarrant too. 'You're an amazing gambler,' he said with a wicked grin as he handed Mark his cheque. 'Can I come in your plane?'

'Avenues and Alleyways', sung by Tony Christie, was the theme song to which Seventies TV series?

♦ A: The Pallisers   ♦ B: The Protectors

♦ C: The Persuaders   ♦ D: The Professionals

FIVE

THE SELECTION PROCESS

t sounds easy. It *is* easy. When the lines open for a new series of *Millionaire* (lines are only open prior to and while the series is on air) you can phone 09002 44 44 44* and a pre-recorded message will ask you which day you'd like to participate in the show, then you'll be asked a multiple choice question and if your answer is correct you'll be asked to leave your name and telephone number. That's all you have to do. If you're selected, you'll be called back before the show you want to be on; you'll be told that the computer has selected you and approximately 99 others to go onto a shortlist and then you will be asked another question. This time it's a 'nearest to' question along the lines of 'What is the length in feet of the QEII?' – and you're only given twenty seconds to answer. If your answer is one of

the ten nearest to the correct one you will have made it to the last stage – you'll be a contestant. You will be called back on the evening before your show is recorded, asking you to come to London.

And there's no way to crack the system. Someone – who had better remain nameless – suggested that if they drove to a poorer part of the country and phoned from there, would they have a better chance of getting on the show? The answer is that they would be wasting their petrol (as well as their time). It doesn't matter if you phone from Bradford or Buckingham Palace, Mayfair, Minehead or

What you see is what you get. The cheques that Chris Tarrant signs on screen are real.

a mobile. Anyway, no one knows who you are or where you're calling from. The initial selection process is randomly generated. Furthermore, it is not organized by *Millionaire*'s production company Celador. That task is undertaken by chartered accountants KPMG and Broadsystem, the largest service provider in the UK, who have created an enormous network to handle the telephone calls.

And the phone line was called rather a lot during the first three series of *Millionaire* (including the Christmas Special in 1998): 10, 143, 915 times, to be precise. That's roughly 150,000 calls per day. And if anyone who called found that the line was busy, they may be in for a shock – every single one of the 4,800 lines dedicated to that number was actually busy ...

It's a Saturday morning, the show is in mid-run, and the lines at Broadsystem are buzzing. All the calls are answered by a network of automated lines. Account manager Siobhan Schafer points to what look like amplifiers. '*They're* answering the phones.' Closer inspection reveals a huge array of screens, with numbers and letters flickering away, displaying a whole bunch of .... well, information.

'Those are the calls in progress,' Siobhan explains. 'The main point is that everything is being digitally recorded; the answers to the questions, the preferred show-date, the name and number of the caller and the duration of the call – which is never

Phoning a shortlisted candidate. Not long ago, the computer selected that candidate. Barely 24 hours from now, he could be a millionaire ...

more than two minutes', says Siobhan. The details of approximately one hundred callers who answered the initial telephone question correctly are short-listed for each day. Callers can dial as many times as they want – but there's no point in calling back having researched the answer to the question as there are large banks of questions which are regularly changed. Interestingly, provision is also made for those potential contestants who fail to specify which programme they are entering for, but still answer the question correctly. A certain amount of these contestants, described as 'defaulters', are allocated randomly – to specific programmes. Then the details of the short-listed candidates are faxed by KPMG to a secret location. There's a special selection team which telephones each of the short-listed candidates and asks them all a 'nearest to' question such as 'How much did 'Seattle Dancer, the most expensive racehorse in the world, cost in pounds when it was sold in 1985?' Contestants are allowed twenty seconds to answer – no time to look it up in an encyclopedia or on the Net. The callers with the ten closest answers will go through to take part in the show. They are informed that if they have been successful they will be called up to 6.30pm on the day before the recording of the show; giving them, in effect, a mere twenty-four hours' notice.

The production team for *Millionaire* don't have much more notice than the contestants themselves. By 6.30pm the contestants have been confirmed and a fax with the names and numbers of the people who gave the closest answers (ie the contestants) is sent to the travel team who immediately set about making the travel arrangements. A further ten names – the next set of 'closest to' answers – are also supplied. The standby contestants will be drawn from the second list. 'There are only ever two standby contestants taking part in each show,' says production co-ordinator Maria Knibbs, 'but some people don't want to be standbys. That's why we need to have more people to call.' Furthermore, some of the first ten may suddenly find they aren't available (to win £1,000,000? They must be mad...) so in that case the standby list is used for a 'real' contestant.

So – no one on earth knows the identity of the final contestants for any show until twenty-four hours before the show itself. And certainly not the contestants themselves – the very people who could be struggling one day and millionaires the next ...

Note: The above describes the selection process in a nutshell. A more detailed explanation is contained within the rules of the competition which are available from the following sources: page 375 on ITV Teletext (a detailed summary), on the programme's web-site – www.phone-a-friend.com and *Who Wants To Be A Millionaire?*, P.O. Box 4444, London WC2E 9TA (please include an SAE).

'What's going on behind me?!'
A happy couple celebrate.

How to make your bid to win £1,000,000:
Chris Tarrant in an early publicity shot.*

* The number has since changed to 09002 44 44 44.

SIX

THE WINNERS: MIKE STOKES

Here's a spooky story. Mike Stokes told *Millionaire*'s researchers that with one million he and his wife Alison would tour Australia, taking Billy Connolly with them. The contestant after Mike, June Woods, had said exactly the same thing (although she and Billy would, of course, be taking her husband and not Alison Stokes). Later the two compared notes and found that they shared the same birthday and, while now living at opposite ends of the country, they were born within a few miles of each other. Even spookier, Billy Connolly has recently bought a house in Aberdeenshire – within a few miles of Mike's house!

Or rather, Mike's old house. In March, Mike won £32,000 on *Millionaire* and used most of the money for the deposit on a new house, The rest, he says, has gone on a new car, paying off debts, and his children. It's all gone now, apart from '£2,000 in the bank for a rainy day'.

And Mike Stokes knows all about rainy days. In January 1998 he lost his job in Essex and, on a wing and a prayer and the £80 they had left in the bank, he and Alison moved to Scotland. There was no immediate prospect of a job, but at least they'd be near two of their daughters.

Then came *Millionaire*. 'I can't remember the question I was asked when I phoned, but when they phoned back with the 'nearest' question it was: "By what majority did Tony Blair win his Sedgefield seat at the General Election?" Well, I answered twenty-seven thousand and then completely forgot about it. I didn't think for one minute that I'd be on the show, let alone become a hot-seat contestant.'

How wrong he was. A few days later, he received a call one evening to tell him he *was* on. Exactly twelve hours later he and Alison left home for the flight south and, exactly twelve hours after that, Mike won Fastest Finger First and found himself in the hot-seat. 'I was the only one who got the question right,' he recalls. 'It was about who won the World Cup most times and I thought I hadn't a hope – the man next to me was the manager of a football club! He said to me "I'm really going to get it in the neck at work ...".'

Mike won £2,000 on his first night and 'rolled over' the next day to accumulate £64,000 – with the help of his Phone A Friend Neil Grafton. Mike used tha lifeline when asked what the first 'A' in NASA stood for (Neil was "110% sure it was Aeronautics.") 'What was *really* strange,' remembers Alison, 'is that Neil hac said "space is my thing. If you get a space questior then ring me".' Given the enormous number of ques tion categories, it was highly unlikely that Mike woulc get a space question. But as we know, anything car happen on *Millionaire*...

It's probably just as well Mike used Phone *A* Friend on that question: one can't imagine anyone having a friend who would say 'Lace is my thing. I you get a lace question then ring me.' And Mike *dic* get a lace question, so he asked the audience for advice on which item was produced in both Honitor and Nottingham. 92% of them said 'Lace'.

'That,' says Mike later, 'is my one regret. wasted a lifeline. I asked the audience a questior about which I was 99% sure of the answer. They merely confirmed what I thought.'

Mike had only one lifeline left – and he needec it. The £125,000 question is shown opposite. The 50:50 lifeline narrowed the options to Jimmy Young and Eamonn Andrews – but Mike was none the wiser You could have heard a pin drop in the studio as he agonized over his decision and, finally, chose Jimmy Young. It was the wrong answer. Despite the fact that according to Chris Tarrant, 'Shifting, Whispering Sands' was 'the worst record I've ever heard,' Mike went down to £32,000, finding himself in the peculia position of hearing the best – and the worst – news at exactly the same time. 'I feel like I'm floating,' he said at the time, referring to the £32,000 he'd wor

Who had a 1956 top twenty hit with "Shifting, Whispering Sands"?

◆ **A: Bill Cotton**

◆ **B: Jimmy Young**

◆ **C: Eamonn Andrews**

◆ **D: Hughie Green**

But – of the £32,000 he'd lost – 'part of me is really hacked off.'

Months later, he's still wondering 'what the £250,000 question would have been and why I didn't take £64,000. But, he adds, 'it was my fifteen minutes of fame and I thoroughly enjoyed every minute of it.'

Anything else?

'Yes. If I wasn't so in love with my wife I could easily have fallen for the researcher who looked after me.'

In common with most of the other *Millionaire* winners, Mike is still being recognized. 'Five weeks after the show,' he recounts, 'I was booking a venue for my daughter's eighteenth birthday and the woman there said "Don't I know you from somewhere?"'

So did Mike let on where she knew him from?

'No!' he says with a laugh. 'She might have put the price up!'

There's one more spooky thing about Mike's win. A few minutes after the show ended, he confessed to Alison that he'd had a dream six weeks previously; a dream that he'd won £16,000. 'I didn't know *how* I'd won it, just that I had.'

So: a word of advice for would-be contestants. Dream on. After all, the only inaccuracy about Mike's dream was that it was £16,000 short of the mark...

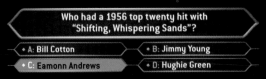

Who had a 1956 top twenty hit with
"Shifting, Whispering Sands"?

◆ A: Bill Cotton   ◆ B: Jimmy Young

◆ C: Eamonn Andrews   ◆ D: Hughie Green

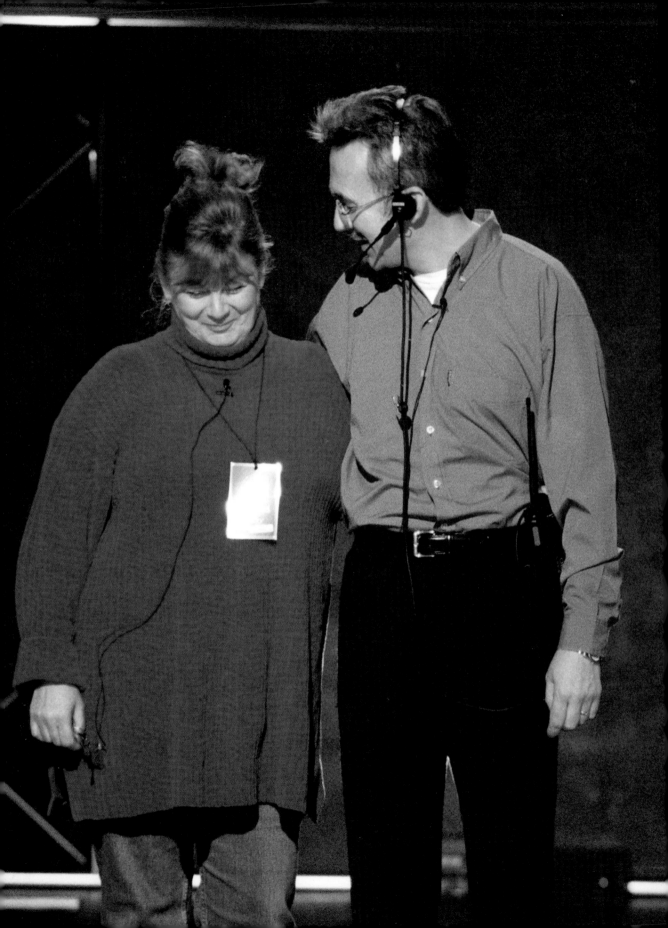

SEVEN

LIVE BEHIND THE SCENES

The rehearsal

'I'll pretend to be Chris Tarrant and you pretend to look happy.' This is producer Colman Hutchinson, on set, addressing tonight's contestants. They don't, in fact, look particularly unhappy – just a little shell-shocked and slightly apprehensive.

It's not surprising. Less than twenty-four hours previously, they received a call informing them that their bid to appear on tonight's show had been successful, that their travel arrangements had been made, and that they were required to be at Elstree Studios in Hertfordshire by 2pm.

It's 4pm. The contestants have come from all over the country (one has flown from Aberdeen) and they haven't had a chance to relax since they arrived. Each, with his or her companion, has been met by the member of the Celador research team. They've been shown to their dressing-rooms and handed information packs. They've also had a chat with associate producer David Briggs and/or scriptwriter Richard Easter to discuss the personal details that may eventually translate into Chris Tarrant announcing: 'Dave from Devon whose wife is expecting triplets in ten minutes and is in the audience right now...' (That's a fabrication but the number of male contestants who have had pregnant wives in the audience is, in fact, quite extraordinary.)

And now they're on set, beginning the rehearsal. As Colman Hutchinson later said, 'The really strange – and unique – thing about this show is meeting the contestants only hours before recording starts. It adds to the spontaneity, to the immediacy of the show. It's one of *Millionaire*'s greatest strengths – and potential weaknesses. If someone appears unsuitable ... well, that's just tough.'

Most contestants also find it rather strange. And, if nervousness counted as unsuitability, it would be really tough for half of tonight's hopefuls. But that's the whole point of rehearsals: to soothe nerves and familiarize contestants with the whole set-up. It's one thing seeing the *Millionaire* set on TV – quite another experiencing it in person.

The first part of the rehearsal (after Colman has made his plea for happiness) involves the contes-

Producer Colman Hutchinson pretending to be Chris Tarrant.

tants holding up their outfits for tonight so the camera can check them for colour and suitability. 'A lot of people *will* insist on bringing the only colour they've been told not to,' sighs wardrobe assistant Billy Kimberley.

And exactly what colour would that be?

'Black.'

So – be warned.

But none of tonight's contestants are hell-bent on appearing entirely in black (it's difficult to light black properly if you're recording on video) and all outfits are deemed suitable.

'Right,' says Colman when everyone's back in place. 'Let's meet our contestants for tonight.'

Tarrant-like, he introduces them one by one. The atmosphere is beginning to thaw: but not the temperature – it's freezing.

Then it's on to rehearsing Fastest Finger First. This is vital. On the contestants' panels are the self-explanatory buttons A, B, C, and D; a Delete button in case a mistake is made; and an OK button. 'You *must* press the OK button,' urges Colman, 'because that's the one that sets the timer. And make sure you press the buttons hard.' Several contestants, to their shame and disappointment, have come a cropper by forgetting Colman's advice about the OK button.

Further hints follow. 'Don't be afraid to lose your lifelines and please remember that when Chris Tarrant says "Are you sure?" he's not trying to put you off; he's trying to make absolutely *sure* you're sure.' This is completely true. Chris Tarrant's constant

The outfits are auditioned. Contestant June Woods (right) holds her winning number.

– and often criticized – refrains of 'Sure?' and 'Final answer?' are crucial. He can't afford *any* element of doubt about an answer that, in the most extreme case, could lose a contestant £468,000.

Then, rather to the surprise of the contestants, Chris Tarrant himself appears. By chance, he has actually been watching for some time from the gallery above; now he comes and sits at the podium.

Apart from the fact that he's wearing jeans and trainers and drinking Pepsi, he's exactly the same Chris Tarrant as the televised version: friendly, chatty – and concerned. 'Sorry if I'm sounding schoolmasterly,' he says after repeating Colman's advice about life-lines, 'but the chair [the hot-seat] is incredibly high

and can be difficult to get into. They can edit out ungainly seating arrangements but let's practice doing it anyway.'

And then they're off; each contestant (including the standbys who are ready to step in as a contestant in case anyone fails to turn up, chooses to back out or becomes ill) practises getting into the hot-seat, answering questions, and choosing lifelines.

The questions asked in rehearsal are similar in format to the 'real' ones, but they are in a separate category. 'We try to make the rehearsals as close as possible to the reality' says Paul Smith, 'so we don't ask questions that have been used in previous shows. All the rehearsal questions are new to the contestants.'

But not to the rehearsal audience. Said 'audience' consists of members of the production crew (up to sixty of them) doing whatever it is they do, as well as the likes of visitors from ITV, guests, Chris Tarrant's children, the writer of this book – and the contestants' partners.

Apart from the latter group, everyone else is familiar with the rehearsal questions and, in this case, familiarity breeds comedy rather than contempt. Ask The Audience provokes hilarious – and largely unprint-able – remarks from Chris Tarrant while the 'friend' contestants phone is a lighting technician who manages to reduce everyone to stitches – and occasionally provide an answer – within thirty seconds.

But there's a serious side to all this. The more nervous the contestant, the more outrageous Chris Tarrant becomes – making them laugh is a highly effective way of calming those nerves. He's probably doing it subconsciously, but his primary motivating factor is to put people at ease. It's what Chris Tarrant does. And that's probably why he was the first, last and only personality ever considered as the host of *Millionaire*.

'He doesn't actually *have* to be at the rehearsals,' says Paul Smith. This, presumably, means that his presence there isn't stipulated in his contract. That's standard: there are loads of quiz show hosts – some of them extremely famous – whose acquaintance with their guests extends to nothing more than a brief 'hello' behind the scenes just before the cameras start rolling. Chris Tarrant, however, is rather surprised by the notion that he needn't be there. 'It's very important that I relate to them, that I help relax them. Let's face it: £32,000, £16,000 – even £8,000 is an awful lot of money. The rehearsal gives me quite a good indication of what people are like, of how far they're likely to go.'

The other, perhaps more surprising aspect of rehearsals is that, despite the informality, the lack of audience and the fact that the cameras aren't rolling – it's almost spookily like the real thing. The lights, camera angles and music are being tested – and even in a cold, empty studio that extraordinary music sends a shiver down your spine. But the contestants themselves provide the best theatre. They're so caught up in the whole scenario, so tense, so anxious to answer correctly that most people completely forget it's only a rehearsal. Later, one woman gives her husband a royal dressing-down for getting a question wrong; several people start a serious post-mortem; and one man admits that 'it's the aftermath you're worried about. You're sitting there thinking "Oh God, what if I only win £200? What'll my mates say afterwards at work?".'

The adrenalin has started to flow. Soon, it'll become a tidal wave...

Pyrotechnic operator David Vialls. He's been waiting a year to light fireworks for the first millionaire ...

The show – as seen by the audience

The audience, who booked tickets through Powerhouse Film and Television (the largest audience ticketing agency in the UK) have been here for some time now. Seats are given out on a 'first come, first served' basis – and some people came at five o'clock to start queuing outside the studio. Shortly after six o'clock the ushers started showing them to their seats. Now they are waiting in eagerness for the action to begin.

Audience tickets are free – but space is restricted. The set seats 220.

Big Brother is watching all the time. Some of the cameras are scanning the audience, not the contestants.

'... and a word of warning for the people sitting facing the podium. Don't jump up and down during recording: you're in danger of being decapitated by the camera crane!' floor manager Griff Evans isn't entirely joking. The people he's addressing look warily behind them. Sure enough, the camera crane lurks above, looking like a refugee from the set of *Alien*. Later, concertina-like, it expands and swoops down towards the podium. It gets within inches of the perspex floor and, from below, takes close-ups of contestants as they agonize over questions.

Eight cameras in all (only one on a crane) record the show; some poised to capture the audience; others different angles of the contestants, the set and Chris Tarrant. But only the one on the crane is intrusive: the rest are tucked away.

Warm-up man Ray Turner making a new friend.

After the talk of decapitation, everyone forgets about the cameras. There's too much going on. For a start, they're *here* – on that famous set that looks like a cross between *Star Wars* and a gladiator's arena. 'It's smaller than on TV, isn't it?' says one woman, seemingly forgetting that both she and the set *are* on TV. But she has a point: nearly everyone expects it to be bigger. Perhaps it looks small because of where it is – smack in the middle of an enormous and otherwise empty film studio. In fact, for a quiz show set, it's huge and extremely elaborate – even if it does only seat 220. But there are more than 220 here tonight and the overflow, along with guests from ITV, are seated in the VIP area behind the set, where they can watch the show on a giant screen. Some of them are grumbling about this – but

not for long. After Griff Evans finishes his safety instructions, on comes warm-up man Ray Turner. He's hilarious, talking nineteen to the dozen, cracking jokes, insulting the camera technicians – and picking on members of the audience. Then he sits in Chris Tarrant's seat. 'You've just won *£32,000!*' he screams in a spot-on imitation of Chris (nearly all the crew on *Millionaire*, in fact, can do a perfect imitation of that). The audience roars with laughter.

Then two men come and take Chris's seat and the podium away which were set up for the rehearsals earlier, they lift the latter, disconnecting cables and putting what looks like a manhole cover in its place.

That's when you realize, 'Of course ... the podium isn't there when they do Fastest Finger First. Someone has to physically remove it and return it (with Chris's seat and the hot-seat) each time a contestant is chosen. For this reason recording a half-hour programme can take up to an hour.

Now Ray picks on a woman in the audience sitting with an enormous handbag on her knee. He bounds up to her and picks up the bag. 'Yuk! It's wet!' he exclaims in disgust. The woman starts to giggle. 'I know. We went to McDonalds beforehand and I put my bag in the basin and the tap turned itself on...' More laughter and a few unprintable remarks from Ray. Then he's off again, cracking jokes and picking on other members of the audience. (There is, in fact, a very good reason why he, followed by the cameras, scans the entire audience. More of which later...)

Then he gets everyone clapping, making sure that what started as a tentative ripple ends up as an enthusiastic roar.

The contestants come and take their seats just before seven o'clock; floor assistant, Susie Charrington looks after them – gives them glasses of water and makes sure they're comfortable. It's much warmer now – and something strange has happened. Not many people notice, but a thin film of odourless smoke has filled the entire set...

Then Chris Tarrant strides in. Like some dynamo, he's all over the place, chatting and making jokes, rushing off to the VIP area to talk to members of the audience who feel left out. (He'll spend a lot of

Every time a contestant leaves the hot-seat, the podium has to be taken away for the Fastest Finger First round. Either Chris Tarrant or Ray Turner will entertain the audience while this is going on.

Floor assistant Susie Charrington gives last-minute advice to Fastest Finger First contestants: 'Don't forget to press the OK button after you've made your selection ... not the delete button!' The fastest finger in this round belonged to £32,000-winner Mark Mills (second from left).

time here during the breaks in recording while the podium is being removed.)

And then, suddenly, it's happening – and it's *exactly* like it is on TV – but with added tension. There's a thunderous – almost deafening – burst of music, accompanied by applause as Chris Tarrant walks in and introduces the show. Then, lightning-quick, he introduces the contestants, shouting out their names above the music and applause. It's straight on to Fastest Finger First – and that's when you realise the genius of the lighting as well as the music. The main lights dim and an arc of little ones

beam down on the contestants, isolating them – putting them, literally, under the spotlight. That's also when the thin film of smoke becomes apparent. Lighting director Brian Pearce later explains that 'you wouldn't actually see the lights properly if it weren't for the layers of smoke.' And audiences may be amused to know that they're partly responsible for the smoke. 'There's a little generator bubbling away at the back of the studio,' explains Brian, 'filling the entire space. But the smoke really needs warmth to get going. When the audience comes in their body heat warms it up...'

But nobody is – consciously – interested in the lights or the smoke. They're looking at the contestants as they choose their answers. They're probably not consciously listening to the music either – but they'd notice it if it wasn't there. It's almost *always* there in *Millionaire* – far more than anyone realizes. As they wait, it's there in the background: a subtle sound like a heart-beat. Increasing the tension. Then, as Chris Tarrant announces the winner, it changes to the familiar flourishing crescendo that is one of the programme's hallmarks.

Then Chris and the successful contestant – a pilot called Mark Mills – disappear while the podium is brought in. Ray Turner comes bouncing in, firing jokes, innuendoes and insults, keeping the momentum going until Chris and Mark return.

What happens now is interesting – and unknown to the audience. An autocue script is being written, ready for Chris to introduce Mark Mills to the audience. And it has to be done at lightning speed. Richard Easter, the scriptwriter, has already met Mark, and Mark has filled out a questionnaire. Similarly, Chris Tarrant has met Mark briefly and, after the rehearsal, discussed – with Richard and David Briggs – what he might say about the contestants. Richard has drawn up a prompt card for each contestant (Chris keeps them to the right of his screen – you can sometimes see him glancing at them). But, until now, no one knew that Mark was going to get into the hotseat. There is no time to write an autocue script for each contestant beforehand. Furthermore, there's no point. If, for example, something unexpected had happened during Fastest Finger First; eg the question was about horses and the winner turned out to be a jockey it would make sense to put this in the autocue script so that Chris could mention it. Just another example of how everything on this show has to be slick, professional – and last-minute.

Mark Mills is pretty slick and professional too. He's up to £1,000 before you know it – and when he gets there you realize something else as well. When he answered the first four questions correctly there was only a tiny ripple of music: when he answers the fifth for £1,000 the lighting suddenly brightens and there's a huge burst of sound. The 'heart-beat' music gets progressively louder with each correct answer

as the questions become more difficult – and the lighting gets progressively dimmer.

Mark gets to £16,000 without using any lifelines. He's generating an enormous amount of tension – from seemingly doing nothing. He's hardly moving, sitting hunched in his seat, looking at the ground. It makes for fantastic TV – but then so do some of the contestants who shout, scream and shake. Another reason why the show is so successful: nobody knows what people are going to do when they get into the hot-seat – except provide an excellent slice of unscripted real life.

Then Mark answers the question for £32,000 and, to a collective gasp from the audience, Chris Tarrant announces that 'You'll find out after the break if you've won £32,000!'

As everyone knows, the show is 'as live' and not 'live': it will be transmitted tomorrow night – but it's kept as close as possible to the real thing. They've recorded about fifteen minutes of the programme so far (if you discount the podium-moving) and it makes sense to break now. That fifteen minutes will be edited down to just over twelve – the standard time for a 'quarter hour' on commercial TV but they must have a natural ending before the commercials. Hence the director tells the floor manager to signal the 'after the break cue' to Chris Tarrant and Mark leaves not knowing whether or not he has won the money – but he's looking pretty confident.

He was right to look confident, and soon he's up to the £64,000 question. He takes a 50:50 – and then agonizes for *ages*. You begin to wonder why he doesn't Phone A Friend: after all, the question was asked three minutes ago. There's plenty of time for the friend to find out the answer. Then you remember: no one on earth outside this studio knows what question has been asked. If he did Phone A Friend, it would be with a question from out of the blue. He doesn't phone. He answers correctly – and then he does something quite extraordinary. He reaches the £125,000 question, he's still got two lifelines – and he doesn't know the answer. But he answers: and gets it wrong. The audience goes wild. Chris Tarrant is alternately admiring and astonished – Mark has chosen to risk (and lose) £93,000 rather than use a lifeline. The applause is thunderous as Chris hands him a cheque for £32,000 and congratulates him on being 'the most memorable bloke yet this series'.

The show – from the director's point of view

'Oh come *on*! I can't believe you don't know the answer. For heaven's sake, man ... it's easy!'

'It's only easy if you know the answer.'

'Oh shut up!'

This conversation, between director Paul Kirrage and producer Colman Hutchinson, is taking place in the outside broadcast unit – otherwise known as the 'scanner'. It's a bit like a portaloo – except that it's smaller. A bank of TV monitors – twenty-nine in all, most of them quite small – makes

up one wall and, for the entire duration of recording, five people sit and look at them.

They are, of course, watching *Who Wants To Be A Millionaire?* They're also making it. The director is doing what his title implies – directing the action. Eight of the monitors show exactly what each of the eight cameras is recording. One, for example, is trained on the contestant's guest, recording her agonized expression. Another is focused on the audience, two others on the contestant from different

Scriptwriter Richard Easter and autocue operator Irena Procyk get to work on a script so that Chris can announce the hot-seat contestant after Fastest Finger First. You'd never guess, but Chris Tarrant will be looking at it (on camera) as he's talking.

angles...and so on. All the cameras are 'mixed' together to make the master tape – and it's the director who decides which camera to cut to and when. But such is the addictive nature of this programme that it's a wonder the people in there remember what they're there to do.

But they do. The contestant over whom Paul is getting tied up in knots makes his choice and suddenly it's all action in the scanner. 'Orange!' shouts Paul into his microphone. A millisecond later one of the monitors – showing the A, B, C, D grid that viewers see on the bottom of their screens – displays an orange lozenge over 'D'.

Then there's a lot of conversation, most of it unintelligible to the layman (well, all right then, to the writer of this book) as the contestant's answer is found to be wrong and he leaves the hot-seat.

But the mechanism by which it is found to be wrong is entirely dependent on Paul Kirrage and his team. The scanner is the nerve centre of *Millionaire*: it's where all decisions are taken about which camera to switch to, when to cue the music – and when to flash the correct answers onto Chris Tarrant's screen.

Audience participation. Each member of the audience – including the contestants' partners – has a little black box.

To put it very simply: if the scanner is the nerve centre of *Millionaire*, then the set constitutes the bits that move: the eyes, ears and limbs in the shape of Chris Tarrant, the camera crew and the floor manager. And then there's the brain: the computer. Elsewhere, locked in a tiny room, is the person who operates it, who sends those orange flashes to the grid and the answers to Chris's screen. Chris Tarrant apart, all these people communicate with each other via 'open talk-back' – microphones and earpieces through which all instructions are relayed.

Paul says 'it's not as complicated as it looks', but we don't really believe him. What is quite simple to grasp is, given the fact that the format of the show is the same every night, most of the camera, lighting and music cues can be pre-planned. 'The direction is always the same for Fastest Finger First, for winning £100, for getting to £32,000 – so we know exactly what to do. What we don't know is who is going to win and how a person is going to react – and particularly how their partner in the audience is going to react.' So they have to be prepared for a husband, wife or friend who might be having a spectacularly televisual nervous breakdown in the audience.

They also have to be prepared for other eventualities. People sitting together in the audience wearing identical shades of the same colour, for instance. Or people wearing clothes emblazoned with logos – which constitutes free advertising. That's part of the reason why, at the beginning of the evening, warm-up man Ray Turner, followed by the cameras does his tour round the audience: it gives the people in the scanner a chance to scrutinize them.

Sure enough, during Ray's warm-up two people were spotted sitting together wearing identical shades of deep blue (which would look odd on camera). Paul asked for one of them to be moved. Then the camera found someone wearing a sweatshirt with a sportswear logo – and Paul relayed to the ushers a request for him to wear it back to front. No shrinking flower, the man stood up in full view of everyone, stripped to his naked torso and turned the shirt round ... only to reveal an even bigger logo. He ended up wearing the shirt inside out.

There are also more urgent considerations – like what shot to start the programme with. If the evening begins with a rollover contestant, Paul might kick off with a look at the money 'tree' showing how much the contestant won the previous night. Then there's continuity: they've got to retake Chris Tarrant reappearing with a contestant if, for instance, his arm isn't draped round his shoulders in the way it was when they left the set.

And then there's the autocue to check for Chris Tarrant's opening. The autocue, a screen of text attached to the camera Chris will be looking at, contains his opening lines. They've only just been written and it's vital to double-check them for any errors. Tonight it starts with a Clinton joke: 'Hillary wants a lengthy divorce while Bill, true to form, wants a quickie.'

The first contestant brings bucket-loads of suspense – and 'shoutability' into the scanner. The

atmosphere becomes electric. Again, it seems surreal that the people sitting on the edge of their seats here are actually making the programme. But they are. Chris Tarrant suddenly goes a bit green (it's the camera, not him) and instructions about filters are shouted into microphones.

The contestant is one Martin Smith, he doesn't know what Lot's wife turned into. Nor does he know what Cherie Blair does for a living: he uses a lifeline for both questions. By £8,000 he's used up all his

It looks like a portaloo from the outside, but it's more Star Trek inside. Vision mixer, Roz Storey (left), director Paul Kirrage (centre) and PA Ali Ratcliffe (right) in the Outside Broadcast Unit.

lifelines and it looks as if it'll soon be over. But a few minutes later Martin is answering (flashed up under Paul's instructions) a question for £250,000 – and you could cut the atmosphere in the scanner with a knife. Paul is shouting at him to 'Go on! *Please* ...' Like everyone else on the crew, Paul would love to see the contestants clear the £125,000 barrier. Martin looks as if he's about to answer ... then changes his mind. He leaves, to thunderous applause, with a real cheque signed then and there by Chris Tarrant for £125,000

– Martin is only the third person in UK television history (all of it made at *Millionaire*) to do so.

At least he's *supposed* to leave with a cheque for that amount. Floor assistant Susie Charrington notices that it's mistakenly been made out for £120,000 and they have to re-shoot Chris's presentation. Martin is so stunned he doesn't seem to notice – or care. Paul, inside his portaloo, issues instructions for the re-shoot.

And whoever thought TV was all glamour?

The show – from the computer room

This is a must for anyone who thinks there may be an element of the show that's 'fixed'. The computer room is the Holy Grail of *Millionaire* – and not just because it's rather difficult to find. It's a small, windowless cupboard tucked away beside the production office adjacent to the set. 'DO NOT ENTER' are the welcoming words on the outside of the door.

At seven o'clock, half an hour before recording, anyone who has been given permission to enter is not allowed out again until recording is finished. Similarly, no one is allowed in after half an hour before recording. And mobile phones are forbidden.

The reason? At seven o'clock questions are downloaded from the computer. The operator instructs it to select a 'stack' of fifteen questions which the first contestant will be asked. Until that point, no one except the people who compile the questions have ever seen them – and even they haven't a clue how the computer will download them. It's all done by a program which selects them according to different levels and categories.

As every night executive producer, Paul Smith, is in the room. So is one of the question compilers (who must forever remain anonymous). And so is Simon Lucas, the computer operator. It's Paul Smith who responds when asked why they download the questions slightly in advance.

'Because we have to check because something may have happened that day to make a certain question inappropriate. Also, there might be pronunciations that we feel Chris Tarrant might not be familiar with. In the latter case, we put a message on his screen prior to the difficult question. Something like "the third word in the next question is pronounced *vor-jack*". It must be rather peculiar for him because, of course, he hasn't a clue that the next question is going to be about the composer Dvorak.'

So the questions are only downloaded to the computer room – not to Chris Tarrant's screen?

'Absolutely. He *never* sees a question until the audience and the viewers see it. It's the same with the right answers. He never sees them until the contestants have made their selection. He may, of course, *know* the right answers – but only in the way you or I would.'

OK, then. How about this: someone who is good with locks breaks into the computer room in the dead of night and, because he's a hacker as well as a burglar, delves into the computer and makes it divulge its secrets. That, surely, could be a method of cheating?

'No,' says Paul Smith. 'For a start, the door has a combination lock. But even if someone manages to enter illegally it would be futile.'

'Why?'

'Because the computer has no data in it except a whole load of numbers that relate to the questions. It needs a floppy disk to actually be able to read the questions.'

And...?

'And there are only two copies of the disk in existence. I take one home every night and' – here he gestures towards the computer – 'Simon takes the other.' Realizing that more stupid questions are about to follow, Paul continues, 'We put them in self-sealing envelopes when the show is finished. Look – you can see ... you ruin the envelope if you try to open it. There's no way you can tamper with them without it being noticed. Anyway,' he finishes, 'the best safeguard has nothing to do with the computer or the questions.'

No?

'No. The best safeguard is that nobody knows who's going to be playing the game.'

This, of course, is true. As if to illustrate that point, the list of tomorrow night's contestants – who have themselves only just been informed that they'll be on the show – has come through from the production office about twenty-four hours before those very contestants are due to be recorded. The only way for them to cheat would be to have a friend in the computer room at this very moment who steals one of the disks, smuggles it out to them (assuming they have a computer which could decode them), tell them to memorize all 2,500 questions for this series overnight, bribe the producer (who decides where the contestants sit) to seat them in, for example, seat two, and then bribe someone else to disable the panels at all the other nine seats after tomorrow's rehearsals so that they would be guaranteed to win Fastest Finger First.

In a word: impossible.

'Our insurers,' says Paul Smith with a dry smile, 'were in here last night. They were more than happy with the arrangement.' So they should be.

Then he turns to the business in hand – recording is beginning. It's Simon the operator who is on 'open talk-back' to the scanner and the technicians on set – and it's surreal watching him at work. There he sits, in front of a perfectly ordinary-looking computer, hand on a mouse, clicking away. It's that click on the mouse that puts the orange lozenge on the chosen question; that organizes some of the music cues; that

sends the questions and answers to Chris Tarrant ... that operates the brain: the computer itself.

Watching from the computer room (there's a monitor beside the computer) is quite extraordinary – mainly because it's the only place in the world where you can see the correct answer at the same time as the question. A little red dot is displayed beside the correct answer on the computer screen and, looking at it at the same time as the contestant below is agonizing over which answer to choose is astonishingly nerve-racking. Especially when, tonight, that contestant is one Davy Young from Belfast.

> *Inside the computer room. You can check in – but you can't check out until the show's over. Paul Smith (foreground) and computer operator Simon Lucas.*

EIGHT

THE WINNERS: DAVY YOUNG

This is what happened when Davy Young was asked a question for £32,000:

'Who are the Jets' rivals in the musical *West Side Story*?' asked Chris Tarrant. 'A) The Tigers, B) The Sharks, C) The Cobras or D) The Pumas?'

'I'll take 50:50,' said Davy, opting to use his third and final lifeline. Then he laughed when the computer left him with a choice between A and B. 'I don't know ... don't know. I would say B but I'm going to take the money.'

'Sure?'

'Yeah. I've had a good time.'

'You've had a very good time.'

'But I'm taking the money.'

'Sure? Taking £16,000?'

'Yeah.' Then Davy laughed again. 'Ah ... why worry. I'll go for it. B.'

Chris Tarrant nearly fell off his chair. 'You lose £15,000 if you get it wrong. You know that?'

'It doesn't matter. It's silly money.'

Which of these garden flowers is named after an 18th-century Swedish botanist?

A: Chrysanthemum

B: Dahlia

C: Poppy

D: Gladiolus

'You're mad, you are.' Then, a moment later, Chris Tarrant added 'You've got a cheque for £32,000.'

Davy's reply was 'I want a gin and tonic.'

It gets worse. The next question was for £64,000, Davy had no lifelines left, wasn't sure of the answer, yet chose to reply.

'Sure?' asked Chris Tarrant.

'No,' laughed Davy, 'but I'll go for D anyway.'

'Final answer?'

'Yes ... no. No. I'll go for C.'

C was the correct answer. And Davy was absolutely sure of the answer to the next question and went on to win £125,000.

Had Davy won £1,000,000 he would have built a house on stilts on the island of Boracay in The Philippines. This so intrigued one of *Millionaire*'s viewers that she later got in touch with Davy and they chatted on the phone for half an hour. Later her husband wrote to him to say that whenever he was next in London he should get in touch and they would take him out to dinner. The lady was from one of the islands near Boracay: her husband was the Filipino Ambassador to the Court of St James.

Davy, typically, is as unfazed by that as he was by winning the money. 'Don't know when I'll next be in London,' he says in his Irish lilt, 'but it'll be fun. We had a great wee chat on the phone. She was a lovely

lady.' Then, practically in the same breath, he goes on to say that 'half of Northern Ireland seemed to be watching as well. Months later I'm still being recognized in bus queues. And one bloke, *totally* plastered – he could hardly walk – came up to me one night and said "I know you. You're on TV," I mean, even in that state he could remember...'

But Davy Young isn't the sort of person you forget. Utterly charming and with a wicked sense of humour, he really does seem to have the 'take it or leave it' attitude he displayed on *Millionaire*. 'Well,' he cautions, 'I'm not normally a risk-taker, 'but I hadn't

arrived with anything, so I wasn't going to lose anything, was I?'

But he was certainly playing merry hell with people's emotions – and Chris Tarrant's sanity. And he might have been throwing caution to the wind, but he was as nervous as hell – 'sweating buckets. I said to the make-up girl "Look, my hand's completely numb, is that normal?" She said "No". I thought I was having a heart attack.'

That was on his 'rollover' night, and might have had something to do with his activities of the previous evening. 'We were taken back to the hotel and I

thought "I'll get a drink. That'll settle my nerves." But I got totally skinned. I got to bed at around 3.30am. Worse still I was wide awake again by 5am. It was terrible ... hopeless.'

A civil servant from Belfast, Davy has been prudent with his winnings. 'But I wanted it in cash,' he laughs, 'not a cheque signed by Chris Tarrant. I said "A cheque from you? I'm not having that ... it might bounce." I asked him if he had a key for that safe thing you see on TV and said that I had a wee plastic bag round the back to put the cash in...'

But the cheque didn't bounce and Davy's invested most of it for his and wife Lynne's retirement. 'But we're also looking for a house for our daughter, we've bought a new caravan and we've been able to pay off the Mini .... do you know the Mini story?'

No.

It turns out that Davy and Lynne are Mini fans and bought one of the last of the Coopers before they changed the design – the day before he was asked onto *Millionaire*. The problem was that Davy had had no intention of buying it: he thought he was only showing it to Lynne. 'She went mad,' he says, 'and offered for it. I was gobsmacked. "Where'll we get the money from?" I asked her.

"It's all right," she said. "I'll pay."

'But *she* didn't have any money.' Davy shakes his head, still seemingly gobsmacked by Lynne's rush of blood to the head. 'Then she just signed a cheque for the deposit.'

The next day (whilst out driving in the Mini) Davy received the call from *Millionaire* telling him he was on. A week later the Mini was paid for.

Davy's got some pretty good advice for would-be contestants: 'Don't take it too seriously. Look at it as a good-time experience. I was having a good time ... and to be honest, I couldn't even remember how much I was going for until the last question. The chap before me,' he adds, 'took it too seriously. I think you've got to be relaxed. I think someone *will* win a million, but only if they're relaxed.'

And it might help them win if the friends they'd chosen for their lifeline were in on the night. 'No one,' says Davy, 'expected me to be there on the Saturday night as well. All five friends were in on the Friday and when I phoned to say I'd be rolling over to the next night as well they said, "Oh, but we won't be here. It's

Saturday Night. We're going out..."' Only Alan Dale stayed in and helped Davy get to £16,000.

Like all the contestants who have benefited from the advice of a friend, Davy has been generous with his thanks. He treated Alan Dale to 'champagne, a meal and a weekend away'. But – again like all the other contestants – Davy had no prior agreement with Alan about sharing any funds he might win. Several people have asked if anyone has drawn up any sort of contract with their friends: the answer, thus far, is a resounding 'no'. It seems that all the friends in need have been friends indeed; they've given their advice because they want to help – not because they want a cut of the money. Long may they continue to do so...

There's still one thing Davy intends to do with his money – buy a dahlia. Read the £250,000 question on p.75 and you'll see why. Davy says, 'I hadn't a clue. Don't know anything about gardening. I don't even *have* a garden. It's all bricks. But I'll never forget now that the answer was a dahlia. I'm going to buy one and look at it every single day – but I haven't found one yet.'

We don't think there's any doubt that Davy will eventually find his dahlia.

Which of these garden flowers is named after an 18th-century Swedish botanist?	
◆ A: Chrysanthemum	◆ B: Dahlia
◆ C: Poppy	◆ D: Gladiolus

NINE

A DAY IN THE LIFE

Who Wants To Be A Millionaire? may only be on the screen for a maximum of an hour – but its production is effectively a twenty-four hour operation. Here is a breakdown of what may happen on a typical day in the life – or life in the day – of the programme:

6am

Patricia Mordecai, director of last night's recording, leaves home for the editing suite in Chelsea. It will take her nearly twelve hours to fine-tune the drama and edit the tape down to within ten seconds of 24'00" for a half-hour programme or 51'00" for an hour special. The final tape has to be biked to the ITV network HQ by 7pm ready for transmission at 8pm. Patricia Mordecai isn't going to see the sun today.

7am

The first of last night's contestants checks out of the hotel. One of Millionaire's researchers is there to assist. He'll do the same for all the contestants.

7.15am

The first of tonight's contestants leaves home (near Aberdeen) to catch a flight to London.

8am

Another Millionaire researcher arrives at the travel office in the Elstree studios. Contestants are advised to phone if they have any problems with their journey – and someone has to man the phones.

9am

An army of cleaners has invaded the dressing rooms, the set, the restaurant and the production offices in readiness for tonight.

Tristan Burt won £16,000.
Chris Tarrant didn't win anything.

10am

Most of the Millionaire production crew – over sixty of them – have arrived. No one yet knows anything about tonight's contestants beyond their names, their ages, where they're coming from and who they're bringing. The producer decides who will sit where on set: they'll separate contestants from neighbouring areas. It would look a bit like 'us' against 'them' if five Scots sat on one side of the entrance and five English people sat on the other side in Fastest Finger First.

Scriptwriter Richard Easter has already scanned the papers and his Dictionary of Dates looking for a topical opening gag for tonight's recording, remembering that it will be aired tomorrow night. He's got to be careful – there will only be one gag and it can't be edited out. It also has to be relevant to the show – not just a joke. One gem from the papers was Rupert Murdoch's birthday: Richard's script for Chris Tarrant was along the lines of, 'a newsvendor I know who's reached the difficult age of sixty-nine. I know he'd like to buy a small place by the sea – Paraguay – so, Rupert Murdoch, give us a call on...' Richard says of the Dictionary of Dates: 'I bought it because I missed a date that would have been perfect – the anniversary of the invention of the telephone.' Oh well...contestants might be heartened to know that not even the production team can win them all...

Paul Kirrage and Patricia Mordecai direct
episodes (appropriately) back-to-back.

10.30am

One of tonight's contestants phones to say he's missed his train. Short panic: it looks like one of the two standby contestants may get lucky. Then the travel researchers find a way of getting him to Elstree on time. Panic over.

11am

The first of tonight's contestants arrives with her husband. (All contestants come straight to the studio – there's no time to go to the hotel.) She's greeted by the researcher who informed her – barely sixteen hours ago – that she would be on tonight's show. The couple are shown to their dressing room and given an information pack detailing the day's schedule.

11.15am

Last night's rollover contestant is the only *Millionaire* contestant left at the nearby hotel (he will be staying there tonight as well). He and his girlfriend go swimming in the hotel pool and plan a leisurely lunch in an attempt to quell mounting panic.

12pm

Several more contestants have arrived at the studios. Some of them are completing the questionnaires they've been given. Amongst others, the questions include: 'Has anything strange or funny happened to you at work?' 'What's the worst job you've ever had?' and 'What's your ideal holiday destination?' Later, Richard Easter and/or David Briggs will visit them to ask more detailed questions in order to build up a

Head of the Millionaire research and travel team, Maria Knibbs organizing a contestant's journey. (Or is she ordering a pizza ...?)

complete profile of them. Everyone is also asked if there's anything they'd rather *not* talk about: the last thing anyone wants is to embarrass the contestants.

One contestant (who hasn't read the welcome pack properly...) asks if he has to stay in his dressing room all day. The answer is 'no'. Contestants are welcome in the bar and restaurant – and the Green Room – a private lounge reserved for the show – is effectively their communal sitting room.

12.30pm

Maria Knibbs, production co-ordinator and head of the research team starts to visit the contestants, checking their ID. Everyone is asked to bring their passport and birth certificate, and perhaps a

Planning journeys. The team has just a few hours to organize twelve journeys so the contestants arrive in time.

marriage certificate – if applicable – and proof of address 'the more the better, really' says Maria. (After all, if you're going to win a great deal of money, they have to know that you're who you claim to be...) Then the Phone A Friend rules and details are confirmed. The contestants themselves phone their nominated friends: they're allowed a maximum of five but must choose only one if and when they need the friend life-line. In the early afternoon, Maria and her team will phone the friends again to check their details are correct and that they are aware of the rules.

1pm

Lunch. A special area of the restaurant is reserved for the contestants. Chris Tarrant arrives. He's been up since 4.30am (doing the day job) so heads to his dressing room for a kip.

2pm

The last contestant arrives. The travel researchers have to ensure that no one arrives later than this. It means the form-filling, the verifications, the choos-ing of friends and the talks with various members of

the crew have to be crammed into two hours before the rehearsal starts at four.

Many of the other contestants are in the Green Room. They've had a chance to get to know each other over lunch and now there's a friendly – if rather nervous – atmosphere.

3pm

On set, final preparations for the rehearsal are underway. Today's director Paul Kirrage is in the outside broadcast unit: the computer operator is in front of his screen; lighting and sound are up and running and the cameramen and the floor manager are in place.

3.45pm

Contestants are ushered onto the set. Their guests are shown to the bank of seats behind the hot-seat – facing Chris Tarrant's chair. They'll sit in the same place tonight – if they were facing the contestants they might be able to nod advice...

4pm

The rehearsal starts with checking how the contestants clothes for tonight – which they hold up against them – will look on camera. If all's well the outfits are taken to the wardrobe department and pressed.

> Audiences are seated on a 'first come, first served' basis – so get there early to be at the head of the queue.

5.30pm

The rehearsal has finished – and the first members of tonight's audience have arrived. They've been fore-warned that seating is on a first-come first-served basis, so a queue is already forming outside the studio. The front-of-house manager is getting ready to greet them, offer them tea or coffee and with the six ushers, to escort them onto the set.

Contestants have gone into make-up. 'Nearly everyone,' says make-up supervisor Cherry Alston, '*loves* being made up. Wives usually stand over their husbands and take photos...'

6pm

Supper and a calming drink in the bar. Chris Tarrant, David Briggs and Richard Easter hold a meeting in the former's dressing room. They go over all the information gleaned from the contestants' forms, from the contestants' conversations with Richard and David, and from the rehearsals. The information will be distilled into prompt cards that Chris Tarrant takes with him to the podium and, when a contestant reaches the hot-seat, for a script for the autocue.

6.30pm

The travel office becomes frenetically busy. The list of tomorrow night's contestants comes through. There are twenty names on the fax: the ten who answered the 'nearest to' phone question most accurately plus the ten who were next in line. 'The second ten,' explains Maria Knibbs, 'are the people we phone to invite as standbys. We need that many because some people understandably don't want to be standbys. Also, some of the selected contestants find they can't actually come – presumably because they thought they were way out with their 'nearest to' answer. (So there's a clue for would-be contestants: if you're shortlisted for the 'nearest to' round don't give up even if you think your answer's completely wide of the mark. Others may be wider...)

Before the fax arrives, no one on the production team has the faintest idea who will appear at the studio less than twenty-four hours from now. And even at this stage, all they know is their names and where they live. Before contacting them, the researchers plan their journeys. 'It's such short notice,' says Maria 'and usually such a shock, that we can hardly ask people to plan the journeys them-

Make-up supervisor Cherry Alston gives Chris Tarrant a make-over.

Chris Tarrant, David Briggs, Colman Hutchinson and Richard Easter discussing contestants before the show in Chris Tarrant's dressing room (below).

selves.' Before 8pm, the researchers must organize those journeys, phone the contestants, convince them that this is no joke and confirm that they will arrive tomorrow. The researchers *have* to confirm the contestants in time for their names to be fed into the computer for Chris Tarrant to announce at the end of tonight's recording.

7pm

The audience is in place.

In London, last night's edited tape arrives at ITV network HQ, ready for transmission in an hour. Director Patricia Mordecai collapses on the sofa.

Paul Smith, a question master and computer operator Simon Lucas close the door of the computer room behind them. They will not be allowed out until recording is finished.

7.15pm

Warm-up man Ray Turner comes on set. Fifteen minutes later Chris Tarrant appears. 'I've whipped them up into a stupor' says Ray. Thunderous applause.

7.30pm

Recording begins with last night's rollover contestant.

7.45pm

That contestant drops out and, with his companion (who could have chosen to stay in the audience) is escorted to his dressing room. A stiff gin and tonic is required – and provided. Later, he goes to the Green Room to watch the rest of the show. A journalist asks if he would mind doing a quick interview and having his picture taken. He'd probably say yes to talking to a wall: he's just won £125,000 and is walking on air.

Later he phones his family to announce the news. They are rather confused. 'But you're on TV *now*,' says his daughter. 'We're watching you.' It's true. They're watching last night's recording. Even the crew find *Millionaire*'s twenty-four hour time-warp rather peculiar. Director of production Steve Springford says 'it's quite possible, in the production

*It's buzzing backstage during the show.
Helen Wood on two phones at once.*

office, to watch what's being recorded on one TV monitor and what's being transmitted on another — and to be watching the same person.'

8pm

The first new contestant wins Fastest Finger First and, up in the travel office, the researchers phone the people she has nominated for 'Phone A Friend' to double-check that they know what might happen if they're contacted. They've already been advised to keep their lines clear between 7 and 10pm. Now they're reminded again that if Chris Tarrant phones later they must have their TV or radio switched off (background interference), that the first person they speak to *will* be Chris Tarrant, and that when their friend comes on the line they will only have thirty seconds to give their answer.

9.15pm

Recording is over. The list of tomorrow night's contestants — which was confirmed barely two hours ago — appears for Chris Tarrant to announce. A couple of shots of Chris Tarrant are retaken as director Paul Kirrage realizes he needs extra footage to make editing possible. (He may have to retake a shot of one of the contestants — exiting the chair, for example — but never of them answering the questions. That element of the programme is, effectively,

live.) Then as the audience filters out, the rollover winner, along with tonight's two subsequent winners, come back on-set to be photographed with Chris Tarrant.

9.45pm

The contestants have left their dressing rooms and are making their way to the bar. The crew and Chris Tarrant do likewise. There are free drinks all round and everyone — even the contestants who didn't manage to take part — is on a high. Several of those contestants say that the whole day has been an extraordinary experience. Adam from Exeter says 'I was expecting it to be quite different ... I thought we'd be shoved away into a corner until we were needed.' So no regrets, then? 'No ... well, I've missed my weekly horse-ride — but it's been worth it.'

So: another successful day on *Millionaire*. Except that it isn't over yet...

10pm

Producer Colman Hutchinson and PA Ali Ratcliffe take over the Green Room and begin a 'paper edit' of tonight's recording: effectively, viewing the tape and writing down the changes that will be made in the edit suite the following day. For an hour's recording, the paper edit could easily last until one in the morning. While director Paul Kirrage has gone home to bed, at 7am the next morning he will duplicate the twelve-hour day that Patricia Mordecai has just finished in Chelsea. And if anyone wonders just exactly what she has been doing all day; here's an extremely simplified version of the editing process:

Although the master tape that is compiled *during* recording (the 'cut to camera seven' sort of lark) theoretically shows the best shot at the best time, subsequent viewing of the eight time-coded tapes from all the cameras will show that at any given second there may be a better shot to insert. Four tapes can be viewed at the same time on a normal TV monitor, using something called a 'quad split'. And while the paper edit involves viewing the tapes and writing down what they're going to do with them: the edit proper involves actually *doing* them – and refining them. And it takes twelve hours working flat out because, for an hour-long show, there may be well over six hundred edits.

So we don't envy Colman Hutchinson and Ali Ratcliffe the task ahead of them. Back to the bar...

10.30pm

Maria Knibbs is seeking out tonight's winners and handing them their cheques. They are, in fact, the same cheques as were signed and handed to them by Chris Tarrant on TV. After recording, they were taken away, checked and the amount confirmed before they were given back to the contestants.

A minibus leaves to take the contestants back to the hotel. Those who aren't staying there – who live close enough to get home tonight – have cars waiting for them.

The hotel guests check in, go to their rooms and then continue the evening in the hotel bar. Some of them have been known to stay there until...

4am

The very hour when *Millionaire*'s host gets up to begin another day. Chris Tarrant – about four hours after he went to bed – gets up in readiness for his morning show on London's Capital Radio.

Three hours later Paul Kirrage starts to edit last night's tape ... and the first of today's contestants begins the journey to Elstree.

Vision supervisor Ian Jones. He's creating the 'master' tape (directly in front of him).

TEN

THE WINNERS: MARTIN SKILLINGS

Cars feature prominently in Martin's family, so it's entirely fitting that, on 9 January, he accelerated to £125,000 in ten minutes flat – a record on *Millionaire*. And he didn't just break the speed barrier: Martin was the first ever contestant to clear the £64,000 hurdle. And the first person on a UK television quiz show to win £125,000.

Even more impressive was Martin's coolness – and the fact that he still had all three lifelines up to the very last question he answered. But, he insists, he wasn't cool at all. 'I was churning butterflies inside. The worst thing is that you think you're going to make a fool of yourself.' The person who informed him that he was going to be on the show corroborates that. 'He was so nervous on the phone he kept saying he wasn't going to come...'

But, on that record-breaking day, the nerves transferred themselves to his wife Miranda. She sat in the audience, alternately shaking, crying, and holding her head in her hands. The following day, says Martin, she had a migraine – and even two months later she hadn't come to terms with their enormous win.

And it couldn't have come at a better time. 'We'd had an awful year,' recalls Martin. 'Our son had a car crash and it's a wonder he wasn't killed; I was fifty and it hit me like an anvil at the back of my head knowing I still had the mortgage hanging over me; we had other worries as well – so much to worry about that we really had forgotten how to laugh.'

So is that why he phoned to try his luck with *Millionaire*? 'No. Not at all. We're actually very private people and it's really unlike us to do something like that. It was Mandy (Miranda) who persuaded me to phone. She was so fed up with me sitting there shouting out the answers so she kept nagging me to phone in. I only made the one call and forgot about it. Then, on Boxing Day, they phoned to tell me I'd been short-

Sir John Hicks was the first British winner of which Nobel Prize?

A: Peace

B: Chemistry

C: Economics

D: Physics

listed. Boxing Day,' he adds with a chuckle, 'is my birthday so of course I thought it was a prank.' It became clear that it wasn't when he was asked what the diameter of the earth was. 'I didn't know, but I knew the circumference so divided it by pi in my head.' (!) His answer was only thirty miles out – and next thing the Skillings' knew was that they were travelling from their home in Brancaster in Norfolk to the *Millionaire* set.

Martin made winning £125,000 look incredibly easy – but then we all know that 'it's only easy if you know the answer' – which Martin didn't when it came

to the £250,000 question. The unlucky question 13, as it happened.

'I'd never heard of Sir John Hicks, so I telephoned a doctor in our village. He didn't answer, and was cut off after thirty seconds. I guessed the answer *wasn't* physics or chemistry or he'd have known, nor Peace, because you tend to know the Peace Prize winner. I asked the audience, but I'm afraid there was no way I was going to trust total strangers with something as big as that.' (74% of them, in fact, gave the right answer.) I *thought* it was economics, but I wasn't 100% sure. If I'd got it wrong I would have lost £93,000 – and you can't risk that. I decided that, at £125,000, my mortgage was taken care of. I'm still delighted with my decision.'

Martin has paid off his mortgage, and, several months down the line, he's still over the moon about it. 'It's a wonderful feeling to wake up every morning and not worry about it. It was unbelievable signing that piece of paper after having that debt hanging round my neck for twenty-five years. It's all thanks to that show. And,' he adds with a grin, 'I've told every-one to enter. I even listen to Chris Tarrant's radio show when I'm in London. To tell you the truth, I didn't really know very much about him before – now I'm terribly impressed.'

So what else has he done with the money?

'Well, I know it sounds incredibly mean and boring, but I've bought a new handle for the cistern and new tiles for the bathroom floor.'

Yes, that does sound rather mean and boring. Nothing else?

Martin grins. 'I bought a PEP just before they finished – and, oh, we've just booked three weeks in the Seychelles.'

That's more like it.

When asked if he could offer any advice to would-be contestants, Martin doesn't hesitate.

'Always listen to the question. It's something an old teacher of mine instilled into me and I've never forgotten it. *Think* about the question before you answer – it's amazing how many people don't. On Fastest Finger First, for instance, I didn't think I had a chance: the question was about arranging parts of a horse in descending order and the chap next to me was a racehorse trainer! Don't know what happened there...'

When Martin won, the show was still being made at Fountain Studios in Wembley. And, if it was out of character for this quiet quantity surveyor to go on *Millionaire* in the first place, he did something even more out of character the next day. 'I went to Wembley Stadium. I love Wembley – I was there when we won the World Cup in 1966 – and stood there between the Twin Towers, leapt in the air and shouted 'Yeeessss!' Then I looked around and felt a bit foolish, but it got it out of my system.'

Most of the money may have gone – but Martin and Mandy have a permanent reminder of it. 'I asked Celador if they could possibly get the original cheque back for us. I was really impressed – they pulled out all the stops and now I've got it, framed in the downstairs toilet!'

Of course, had Martin answered 'Economics', he would now be looking at a cheque for double that amount...

Sir John Hicks was the first
British winner of which Nobel Prize?

◆ A: Peace   ◆ B: Chemistry
◆ C: Economics   ◆ D: Physics

ELEVEN

QUESTIONS MASTERED:

THE QUESTIONS, THE COMPUTER AND THE PEOPLE WHO HAVE THE ANSWERS

Mastermind. Chris Goss, the unsung hero of Millionaire who created the computer programme, pictured during rehearsals.

T here is one man who *does* have all the answers – associate producer and question co-ordinator David Briggs. Sounds like the perfect person to make into your new best friend. Except, of course, he's not telling. He can't. He can't remember them.

No one could. There are about 2,500 questions stored in the database for each new series and, in addition, approximately eight hundred for the 09002 44 44 44* phone line, about sixty for the 'nearest to' questions posed to the shortlisted contestants, two hundred and fifty for the rehearsal questions and hundreds more for Fastest Finger First. And then there are the possible answers...

Of all the above, only the rehearsal questions are used over and over again. 'It's a standing joke on set,' laughs David. 'Everyone's heartily sick of them. I suppose we'll have to do something about it...' But it doesn't matter whether or not they do – there's nothing riding on those questions. (Funnily enough, although most of the crew are familiar with a lot of the rehearsal questions, they keep forgetting the right answers. Incorrect ones seem to stick in the mind as much as correct ones.)

So who, exactly, sets these thousands of questions? Again David Briggs isn't telling. 'We have a team of question-setters – but we're not divulging their names.' So – no fun there for prospective cheats.

But David does divulge the secrets of the whole question-setting process; and it's impressively elaborate. Each question-setter compiles a list of questions and multiple choice answers, checks them against three different sources, hand-delivers them (so it doesn't get into the wrong hands) to another question-setter who checks them again and, in turn, hand-delivers them to David Briggs. Once all the questions for the series are with him, he checks them again and puts them all onto one disk. Then the computer program takes over; cross-referencing all questions, and

No wonder David Briggs looks happy. He's seen the answers to every question.

discarding any identical or similar ones. The program also caters for the following categories: the phone, rehearsal and Fastest Finger First categories, for example, can never be mixed up and are downloaded separately. The questions to be asked on the night remain on disk and are arranged into 'stacks' of fifteen by the program – shortly before they appear in front of the contestants. No one, therefore, knows precisely which fifteen questions will be downloaded.

That's the simple version. Given what's at stake, there are all sorts of safeguards. The compilers, for instance, also supply the level of the question, the category and sub-category, the incorrect answer to be displayed in the event of a '50:50', three points of reference as to the origin and validity of the answer, background information about the answer and the correct pronunciation of any difficult or unfamiliar words. And, as David Briggs points out, 'they have to be absolutely sure not just that the right answer is right, but that the wrong ones are definitely *wrong*.'

So what's all this about 'levels' and 'categories'? And how can you decide a 'level' anyway?

'Deciding on a level of difficulty,' admits David Briggs, 'is very time-consuming – especially when you get to the higher questions. Even there, it's easy if you know the answer.'

True, but given that it's not exactly in the interests of the programme to throw £1,000,000 at someone without them having to display an extraordinary breadth of knowledge, *Millionaire* doesn't make it easy for them. They're also extremely precise about how the questions look. 'We like to think we have a style that identifies them as *Millionaire* questions,' says David Briggs. 'The questions have to be the same length, they have to look good on screen – and the wording is incredibly important. They have to read well and be grammatically correct.'

So do you still think you could win £1,000,000 – try the following sample questions and see how you get on!

Ian Horsewell – three questions away from winning £1,000,000...

09002 44 44 44* Questions

What is a man who makes barrels called?

- A: Mercer
- B: Cooper
- C: Farrier
- D: Smith

Which country's Rugby Union team is nicknamed the 'Pumas'?

- A: Australia
- B: South Africa
- C: Japan
- D: Argentina

What is a Fender Stratocaster?

- A: A guitar
- B: A lawn mower
- C: A fairground ride
- D: A motorbike

What is the correct name for conkers?

- A: Beech mast
- B: Acorns
- C: Sweet chestnuts
- D: Horse chestnuts

The Shortlist

(examples of "nearest to" questions)

1.

The 1990 Grand National was won by Mr Frisk in record time. How many seconds did it take him to complete the Aintree course?

2.

In feet, what is the length of the span of the Humber Estuary Bridge?

3.

By what majority did Tony Blair win his Sedgefield seat at the 1997 General Election?

ANSWERS ON PAGE 128

Put Yourself In The Hot-Seat!

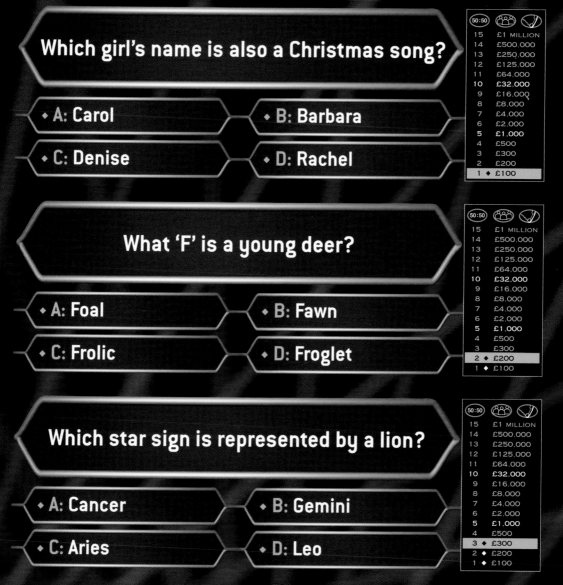

Which girl's name is also a Christmas song?

◆ A: Carol
◆ B: Barbara
◆ C: Denise
◆ D: Rachel

15	£1 MILLION
14	£500,000
13	£250,000
12	£125,000
11	£64,000
10	£32,000
9	£16,000
8	£8,000
7	£4,000
6	£2,000
5	£1,000
4	£500
3	£300
2	£200
1 ◆	£100

What 'F' is a young deer?

◆ A: Foal
◆ B: Fawn
◆ C: Frolic
◆ D: Froglet

15	£1 MILLION
14	£500,000
13	£250,000
12	£125,000
11	£64,000
10	£32,000
9	£16,000
8	£8,000
7	£4,000
6	£2,000
5	£1,000
4	£500
3	£300
2 ◆	£200
1 ◆	£100

Which star sign is represented by a lion?

◆ A: Cancer
◆ B: Gemini
◆ C: Aries
◆ D: Leo

15	£1 MILLION
14	£500,000
13	£250,000
12	£125,000
11	£64,000
10	£32,000
9	£16,000
8	£8,000
7	£4,000
6	£2,000
5	£1,000
4	£500
3 ◆	£300
2 ◆	£200
1 ◆	£100

Which of these is connected with a locker at the bottom of the sea?

◆ A: Davy Jones

◆ B: Peter Tork

◆ C: Michael Nesmith

◆ D: Mickey Dolenz

15	£1 MILLION
14	£500,000
13	£250,000
12	£125,000
11	£64,000
10	£32,000
9	£16,000
8	£8,000
7	£4,000
6	£2,000
5	£1,000
4 ◆	£500
3 ◆	£300
2 ◆	£200
1 ◆	£100

On what day do children demand 'Trick or Treat'?

◆ A: Thanksgiving

◆ B: Hallowe'en

◆ C: Christmas

◆ D: Easter

15	£1 MILLION
14	£500,000
13	£250,000
12	£125,000
11	£64,000
10	£32,000
9	£16,000
8	£8,000
7	£4,000
6	£2,000
5 ◆	£1,000
4 ◆	£500
3 ◆	£300
2 ◆	£200
1 ◆	£100

What line on a ship indicates the safe loading level?

◆ A: Running line

◆ B: Trainer line

◆ C: Wellington line

◆ D: Plimsoll line

15	£1 MILLION
14	£500,000
13	£250,000
12	£125,000
11	£64,000
10	£32,000
9	£16,000
8	£8,000
7	£4,000
6 ◆	£2,000
5 ◆	£1,000
4 ◆	£500
3 ◆	£300
2 ◆	£200
1 ◆	£100

Name the Lone Ranger's horse

◆ A: Tonto

◆ B: Silver

◆ C: Scout

◆ D: Kemo Sabe

15	£1 MILLION
14	£500,000
13	£250,000
12	£125,000
11	£64,000
10	£32,000
9	£16,000
8	£8,000
7 ◆	£4,000
6 ◆	£2,000
5 ◆	£1,000
4 ◆	£500
3 ◆	£300
2 ◆	£200
1 ◆	£100

Name the official who summons MPs at the State Opening of Parliament

A: Black Ron
B: Black Rod
C: Black Roy
D: Black Roger

15	£1 MILLION
14	£500,000
13	£250,000
12	£125,000
11	£64,000
10	£32,000
9	£16,000
8 ◆	£8,000
7 ◆	£4,000
6 ◆	£2,000
5 ◆	£1,000
4 ◆	£500
3 ◆	£300
2 ◆	£200
1 ◆	£100

In poker, what name is given to a hand containing the top five cards in the same suit?

A: Full House
B: Royal Flush
C: Straight
D: Four of a kind

15	£1 MILLION
14	£500,000
13	£250,000
12	£125,000
11	£64,000
10	£32,000
9 ◆	£16,000
8 ◆	£8,000
7 ◆	£4,000
6 ◆	£2,000
5 ◆	£1,000
4 ◆	£500
3 ◆	£300
2 ◆	£200
1 ◆	£100

What does the 'D' stand for in the abbreviation 'L.E.D.'?

A: Device
B: Diode
C: Dynamo
D: Dial

15	£1 MILLION
14	£500,000
13	£250,000
12	£125,000
11	£64,000
10 ◆	£32,000
9 ◆	£16,000
8 ◆	£8,000
7 ◆	£4,000
6 ◆	£2,000
5 ◆	£1,000
4 ◆	£500
3 ◆	£300
2 ◆	£200
1 ◆	£100

Which car company's badge features the astrological symbol for the planet Mars?

A: Skoda
B: Lancia
C: Volvo
D: Chrysler

15	£1 MILLION
14	£500,000
13	£250,000
12	£125,000
11 ◆	£64,000
10 ◆	£32,000
9 ◆	£16,000
8 ◆	£8,000
7 ◆	£4,000
6 ◆	£2,000
5 ◆	£1,000
4 ◆	£500
3 ◆	£300
2 ◆	£200
1 ◆	£100

MILLIONAIRE
107

According to Arthurian legend, which knight threw the sword Excalibur back into the lake?

◆ A: Sir Lancelot
◆ B: Sir Bedivere
◆ C: Sir Percival
◆ D: Sir Galahad

15	£1 MILLION
14	£500,000
13	£250,000
12 ◆	£125,000
11 ◆	£64,000
10 ◆	£32,000
9 ◆	£16,000
8 ◆	£8,000
7 ◆	£4,000
6 ◆	£2,000
5 ◆	£1,000
4 ◆	£500
3 ◆	£300
2 ◆	£200
1 ◆	£100

GBZ is the international car registration for which area?

◆ A: Jersey
◆ B: Isle of Man
◆ C: Gibraltar
◆ D: Guernsey

15	£1 MILLION
14	£500,000
13 ◆	£250,000
12 ◆	£125,000
11 ◆	£64,000
10 ◆	£32,000
9 ◆	£16,000
8 ◆	£8,000
7 ◆	£4,000
6 ◆	£2,000
5 ◆	£1,000
4 ◆	£500
3 ◆	£300
2 ◆	£200
1 ◆	£100

Which American state is known as the "Keystone State"?

◆ A: Pennsylvania
◆ B: Delaware
◆ C: Tennessee
◆ D: New Jersey

15	£1 MILLION
14 ◆	£500,000
13 ◆	£250,000
12 ◆	£125,000
11 ◆	£64,000
10 ◆	£32,000
9 ◆	£16,000
8 ◆	£8,000
7 ◆	£4,000
6 ◆	£2,000
5 ◆	£1,000
4 ◆	£500
3 ◆	£300
2 ◆	£200
1 ◆	£100

Which planet has a moon called Larissa?

◆ A: Jupiter
◆ B: Saturn
◆ C: Uranus
◆ D: Neptune

15 ◆	£1 MILLION
14 ◆	£500,000
13 ◆	£250,000
12 ◆	£125,000
11 ◆	£64,000
10 ◆	£32,000
9 ◆	£16,000
8 ◆	£8,000
7 ◆	£4,000
6 ◆	£2,000
5 ◆	£1,000
4 ◆	£500
3 ◆	£300
2 ◆	£200
1 ◆	£100

ANSWERS ON PAGE 128

Questions That Tripped Them Up

Where was the board game Monopoly invented?

- **A: America**
- **B: Britain**
- **C: Canada**
- **D: Australia**

Which is the oldest weekly publication?

- **A: The *Spectator***
- **B: The *Stage***
- **C: The *Lancet***
- **D: *Old Moore's Almanack***

What was the name of the first American spaceship to orbit the earth?

- **A: *Aurora 5***
- **B: *Liberty Bell 6***
- **C: *Friendship 7***
- **D: *Freedom 8***

What was Casanova's job in his later years?

- **A: Spy**
- **B: Librarian**
- **C: Chemist**
- **D: Soldier**

ANSWERS ON PAGE 128

TWELVE

THE WINNERS: JOHN McKEOWN

'I just wanted to get the first five questions right. I didn't want to go out early and look daft.' John McKeown couldn't look daft if he tried. A strapping six-foot sewage worker, he mesmer-ized viewers as, in Chris Tarrant's words, 'he had the entire nation hanging onto their seats for two nights.' The first-ever contestant to get past question eleven – and the first person in the history of UK television

Which artist has never had a No.1 hit?

A: Genesis

B: Marvin Gaye

C: Fleetwood Mac

D: UB40

to be within four questions of winning £1,000,000 – he eventually left with £64,000. Chris Tarrant was so excited by John's performance that he leaped to his feet and kissed him on the head – not the sort of gesture that the ice-cool Glaswegian is used to! Luckily, John didn't take umbrage – quite the opposite. He and Chris Tarrant ended up in the hotel bar later that night, and made hefty inroads into John's winnings. 'I think he left London with £63,000 instead of £64,000,' said a rather subdued Chris Tarrant the following day.

John's stint on *Millionaire* was a perfect example of the mixture of the agony and the ecstasy of the programme. He reached £64,000 on his first night – and then the buzzer went. He had to endure 'the worst night of my life' before coming back to try and break the five-figure barrier. He had one lifeline left – Phone A Friend – to help him. But in the end, that too proved agonizing. 'I didn't hear my friend's answer to the question [shown above], so I didn't answer myself.' Yet John expresses not the slightest trace of disappointment – he'd come far further than he ever expected. Indeed, he had told his son John (who was in the audience) that he'd 'stop at £4,000.' He didn't, of course – but then he really didn't expect to be asked a succession of questions to which he knew the answers. He demonstrated perfectly that it doesn't matter how well you were educated or what you do for a living, but that a broad range of interests provides the key to success on *Millionaire*. 'I knew Leslie Thomas was the author of the book *Virgin Soldiers* because I'd read it. I knew *Genevieve* was a car because I'd read that book as well – and I knew a frog was the most poisonous creature in the world because I'd watched David Attenborough's nature shows.' The questions that John wasn't sure about, and for which he used his first two lifelines, were about how often the Ryder Cup is played (every two years) and which city is the capital of California (Sacramento).

Like so many other contestants, John thought his summons to appear on *Millionaire* was 'a wind-up'. 'Well,' he says with a grin, 'all I'd done was make one phone call and answer two questions. I'd told my mates that I might be expecting another call, so when it came I was sure it was someone taking the mick.' Well it wasn't – and the next thing John knew, he was in London. And, two months later, he went back to the capital with his wife and both his children. 'We went for a long weekend and I took the family to visit the *Millionaire* studio. Everyone was great. Really welcoming. I'd love to go back again.'

As a visitor?

'No! As a contestant. I'd be there in two seconds flat. And I'd go for the million this time. Definitely. There'd be no pressure on me this time. Anyway,' he adds (in the understatement of the year), 'I don't feel the pressure much.'

The sensible Scotsman has been canny with his winnings. 'OK – £64,000 is a good few years' pay, but it isn't enough to change your life. I've no plans to give up work. I enjoy it. I've been in the building game all my life and the lads are a good bunch.' Apart from holidays in Tenerife, Portugal and Gran Canaria ('I still shop around for a bargain!'), John is in the process of buying his house off the council. 'They're taking their time, though,' he says with a dry smile.

Perhaps it's time to phone *Millionaire* again?

'Oh aye. Definitely. And at least we can pay the phone bill now...'

Which artist has never had a No.1 hit?

A: Genesis

B: Marvin Gaye

C: Fleetwood Mac

D: UB40

THIRTEEN

AN INTERVIEW WITH CHRIS TARRANT

Chris Tarrant is no stranger to quiz shows: he's hosted a whole clutch of them throughout his career, both on television and radio. If the formats have all been different, there has always been a common denominator – people. And, as Chris talks about *Who Wants To Be A Millionaire?*, he's reminded of one person in particular. A man who, years ago, phoned in during one of his radio shows.

'He was this bloke called Jim – an *amazing* man. I never saw him, never met him ... he phoned from the warehouse he was working in and just got on a roll. He kept getting questions right and saying "come on CT, let's go for it". He got up to £6,000 and I was *desperate* for him to take the money but he kept going "One more, CT, one more" and I was saying "No! No! Take it!" and he'd reply "Pressure, CT, pressure!" He then got up to £12,000 and I was *screaming* at him to take the money but instead – I remember this vividly – he tossed a coin ... you could hear the unmistakable noise of a coin being tossed and then Jim saying "We go on!"'

Chris Tarrant pauses for breath (this doesn't happen often) and then adds, 'He made *brilliant* radio. You simply wouldn't have been able to get out of your car if you'd been listening. He got up to £24,000...and then lost the lot. And do you know what he said? "CT, this has been the best morning of my life".

'It was,' finishes Chris Tarrant with a heartfelt sigh, 'the *worst* morning of my life.'

There, in a nutshell, are all the reasons why Chris Tarrant was the only host ever considered for *Millionaire*. He somehow manages to combine the attributes of getting on with people he's never met with kindling their competitive spirit, being both trivial and serious, providing excellent entertainment and, most of all, with genuinely caring about people. Paul Smith of Celador says that 'he has an extraordinary gift ... this ability to be liked by all ages, all classes, both sexes – he's their friend. It's wonderful to see. There's absolutely nothing calculated about him.'

Cynics may well reply 'Yes but you would say that, wouldn't you? You're employing him.'

Well the contestants aren't employing him. Martin Skillings, a contestant in series two, remembers that 'My children wanted his autograph and, to be honest, I was rather embarrassed about asking for it. The last thing I expected was for Chris Tarrant to invite me into his dressing room when he saw me outside, sit me down and give me a drink. His wife was there; his children; some showbiz friends...Then, later that night when I became the first contestant to win a six-figure sum, he came into the bar with some champagne – and his daughter gave my wife and me a carnation each.'

Chris Tarrant himself, however, would shrug off sainthood. He's too normal. He is also, on *Millionaire*, something of a cross between Magnus Magnusson and Robin Hood. So how does he respond to accusations – with his constant 'sure?' and 'final answer?' – that he's also playing Devil's Advocate.

'Look,' he says, 'I would never *ever* want to be the one who lost someone a fortune. I do actually have to know beyond a shadow of a doubt that they're sure. And yes, it is deliberately adding to the tension, but I'm testing people to their limits. That wonderful bloke Davy (Davy Young who won – in an amazing piece of theatre – £125,000); I knew he would go up. But I could *never* say to anyone "Oh go on, it's only eight thousand."'

Then Chris Tarrant repeats his remarks about going to the rehearsals – about how he couldn't imagine *not* going because 'It gives me quite a good indication of what people are like, of how far they're likely to go.'

This is borne out in the daily briefing meeting about the contestants with scriptwriter Richard Easter, David Briggs and Chris Tarrant. Chris Tarrant hasn't spent nearly as much time with the contestants as the other two men – but just enough to give him a 'feel' for them. His remarks are interesting – and usually accurate. 'He seems like a real laugh' or 'she's shy – but I reckon she's as sharp as a button' or 'he'll go for it'. Small, innocuous remarks – but a big clue as to how he'll relate to these people.

'In a way,' he adds, 'I'm doing the same as the viewers are doing at home: looking into people's souls. But I'm seeing them so close up that you can tell exactly what they're thinking. With someone who knows the answer before the choices come up you can see the flicker in their eyes ... I see that a *lot*. Also, if I know, if I genuinely know that they're not going to change their minds then I can tease them a bit. That's why I couldn't and wouldn't do this if I was provided with the answers. People would be able to see it in my eyes.'

You believe him: this is a man who would be totally useless at deception. He just shows exactly what he feels. There's a shot (edited out) from series two when he got so excited about John McKeown winning £64,000 that he leapt out of his chair and kissed John on the head. Chris Tarrant laughs at the

Ian Horsewell and Martin Skillings. The man in the middle is holding cheques totalling £250,000. In one historic night, both men won £125,000.

memory. 'I *was* just so excited. And then I imagined all John's mates in the pub in Glasgow watching and yelling "He kissed him! He kissed him! The man's going to die!". I nearly did die, actually when I went to the hotel bar with John afterwards.'

Chris Tarrant, in fact, appears with the contestants in the studio bar after every show. 'He spends little of this time with us,' says Paul Smith. It's true. He gives all his time, after the show, to the contestants.

One last thing: Chris Tarrant is mad. One night he left the bar at 11 pm, went home and then went fishing for two hours. In the morning, as usual, he had to get up at 4.30 for his Capital Radio show – and then repeat the *Millionaire* process in the afternoon and evening, until 11 pm. 'He's a nutter,' says friend and producer Colman Hutchinson. 'Barking' says PA Ali Ratcliffe with a fond smile. 'But don't put that in the book. He might think we meant it.'

FOURTEEN

THE WINNERS: FIONA WHEELER

'I've had my fifteen minutes of fame – and then some,' says Fiona Wheeler. The 'some' includes interviews with half of Britain's national newspapers, an appearance on GMTV and on the now defunct *News at Ten*, and a live link-up to Australia on the eve of their own *Millionaire* transmission. She's shortly to appear in a documentary about people whose lives have been changed by appearing on TV and, even though she was on *Millionaire* in January 1999, she's still recognized everywhere she goes. Fiona seems slightly surprised by this. No one else is: Fiona Wheeler is unforgettable.

The mother of four from Canvey Island in Essex burst onto our screens with an exclamation of 'I think I've wet meself!' when she won Fastest Finger First. She went on to declare her ambition of 'lying in a bath of melted chocolate' and, in Chris Tarrant's words, to prove herself to be 'one of the nicest, most genuine and most memorable people we've ever had on the show.' Then she screamed and exclaimed her way to £32,000: enough to pay off her family's debts, invest for the future, take a holiday abroad – and to lie in a bath of melted chocolate.

Except it was the *TV Times* who sorted the chocolate. 'When they made my dream come true I wallowed in the chocolate like a little hippo. It was fantastic, really sensuous. I was in there for forty-five minutes with a glass of champagne in one hand and a bar of chocolate in the other. Even after I got it all washed off I still smelt of chocolate and in the car going home I kept getting a lovely whiff of the stuff.'

But Fiona hasn't changed. 'I know I can rabbit on for England,' she laughs, 'but I've always been like that. And I've always been a bit excitable – but I get in the same sort of state over my kids' sports days. I'm bit of an embarrassment to my eldest. He's always saying "Oh Mum, do you have to do that. Everyone at school calls you Screamer."'

Fiona's *Millionaire* screams began the night she was told to expect a call if she'd made it to the final ten. 'They told me that they'd ring between four and six so I sat by the phone, willing it to ring. I'd worked myself up into believing I'd get there but, of course, it didn't ring. Then I got up to make the kids' tea and completely forgot about it. Then they rang and I was so stunned that I couldn't speak.'

So you screamed?

Fiona lets out a great peal of laughter. 'After a minute, yes. I was screaming my head off ... I think I swore down the phone as well. I heard the girl at the other end saying "We've got a screamer here", but I couldn't help it. I was so excited.'

But her excitement palled a bit after rehearsals the next day. 'I loved it all, being in a TV studio and all that, but I made a right bodge of the rehearsal. Couldn't get anything right. I thought "C'mon you dopey cow" but it was useless. So I talked myself out of it.'

So Fiona's shock when she did get on was total. 'All I wanted to do was get the question right and press the right buttons – and suddenly the camera zoomed in on me.' Fiona goes on to explain that when they paused to bring the podium in 'I had to go out and have a fag. I was falling to bits. Chris Tarrant was going "come on, enjoy it" so I said "how can I? I can't even stand up ..." When we did go on, God knows what people must have thought. They must have thought "poor girl, they've let her out for the day."'

It turned out to be more than a day. The buzzer went when Fiona reached £1,000 and she rolled over to the next night. 'I was a shivering wreck all night. I woke at 4am convinced that one of the next questions would be about Queen Victoria's death. There I was on the bog with a fag, going through the reference books. It was 1901, but of course they never asked it.'

The following night Chris Tarrant introduced Fiona – in something of an understatement – as 'an excitable girl' – and she didn't disappoint. By the time she'd reached £8,000 she had screamed, shouted, punched the air with a fist, practically chewed her lip raw and urged herself to 'come on girl, come on!' Chris Tarrant remembers that 'the sheer, genuine emotion was extraordinary. I was watching this wonderful woman and it was all there, written on her face. You could see she was thinking "that's the credit card bill paid off ... that's a holiday for the kids. It was absolutely genuine. Absolutely wonderful.'

But, when Fiona reached question 9, things looked like getting a little less wonderful. The question was 'Which character was played on screen by Jay Silverheels?' and, with only one lifeline left, Fiona phoned her father-in-law Dave Wheeler. He seemed in very little doubt as to the answer, saying 'it was C, Tonto.'

Fiona didn't seem convinced. 'Are you sure?'

'Yes.'

'Definite?'

'Yes.'

'Honest?'

'Yes.'

'Really?'

'*Yes.*'

Fiona turned to Chris Tarrant and proudly announced, 'That's my father-in-law,' – and promptly won £16,000, then £32,000.

Fiona's lavishness with her emotions extends to her gestures. As a 'thank you' she took her parents-in-law, along with husband Matthew and all the children on holiday to Kos. 'First time on a plane for the kids.' At Christmas, she, Matthew and the children are going skiing. 'I'm going for a laugh. I've always wanted to ski but I'm not sure I'd be very good at it. And I'm probably too old to learn.'

Rubbish – she's only thirty-three.

'I'm not sure where we'll go,' she muses. 'It was going to be Bulgaria but I don't like the look of things there now. Still, wherever we end up I'm sure there'll be trouble: there'll be someone saying "Oh God, that mad woman from Essex is on her way..."'

The question that stumped Fiona was for £64,000 and, as Fiona debated with herself, the audience silently egged her on. 'We've got a Test ground called the Oval but that's in Kennington. Must be Australia. The Australians nick everything of ours so it must be them ... on the other hand so does Jamaica. Or is it Barbados?'

By this time, half the audience – and Chris Tarrant – were on the edge of their seats. An awful lot of them (Chris included) knew the answer – but Fiona doesn't watch cricket. 'Test matches?' she says later. 'You think I've got time to watch Test matches?' Another great peal of laughter. 'I've got four kids, I've got the ironing, the cleaning...'

Eventually, Fiona chose Jamaica – the wrong answer. 'I don't care,' she announced as Chris Tarrant hugged her. 'I don't care.'

And she didn't.

Which country has a Test cricket ground called Kensington Oval?

♦ A: England

♦ B: Australia

♦ C: Jamaica

♦ D: Barbados

Her win came at the end of a bad year. She'd written the car off in a crash, suffered from whiplash and 'Matthew had to take time off work to look after me, so I was wondering how we would pay January's bills.' Matthew, she goes on to say, often had to work seven days a week – he's an electrician – to meet those bills, so the win really took the pressure off. 'We weren't on the breadline,' she says, 'but there wasn't exactly money sloshing about.'

After the show, Chris Tarrant wrote to her to tell her she was mad, that he'd had enormous fun, and to thank her for coming on the show. 'Well,' remembers Fiona, 'that was when there was a bit of a media frenzy and they were taking photos of me stuffing my face with chocolate. So I wrote back enclosing a photo and saying "don't you think I look like Kate Moss here?" I really didn't expect him to reply, but he did – wrote back saying I'd brightened up his morning.'

So is the correspondence continuing?

'No.' Fiona giggles. 'He's a really lovely man, but I really don't want to turn into one of those weird women who stalks the stars. One of them stalky-bits.'

But, Fiona, stalkers are supposed to operate by stealth ... A silent, stealthy Fiona Wheeler is quite impossible to imagine. Anyway, things have happened almost the other way round – it's Fiona who's being stalked by the media.

'But I love it,' she says. 'It's been so much fun. It hasn't changed me one bit, but I have to say I love the attention. It hadn't changed my life, and nor has the money. It's been enough to pay off the credit cards, invest a tidy sum and pay for two holidays. When you've got four kids some things are beyond your budget. You can't clear your mortgage and you can't change your life, but you can make it easier. It's a wonderful feeling.'

So would she do it again?

'In a heartbeat. I'd be there in a flash. I know I told Chris Tarrant that I'd sooner have a baby than appear on the show, but that was just nerves. D'you know,' she adds, 'you do go into shock. I mean, some people get stunned and just sit there and nod. I s'pose that's the wonderful, exciting thing about the show; they're just ordinary, everyday people. I'm living proof of that ... a normal, everyday housewife who cleans the cooker, does the ironing and takes the kids to school. I used to think things like that never happened to people like me – but they do.'

You wonder, however, if there's anything that could happen that could stun Fiona into silence.

'Oh there is,' she laughs. 'I took one of the kids to the doctor yesterday – I mean this is *months* after the show – and I asked the doctor what he thought was wrong with him. The doctor replied "I don't know. Can I phone a friend?"'

Which country has a Test cricket ground called Kensington Oval?

◆ A: England	◆ B: Australia
◆ C: Jamaica	◆ D: Barbados

Are You Sure?

Test yourself on your favourite show

Your initial call to *Millionaire* will last no longer than

- A: Thirty seconds
- B: Two minutes
- C: One minute
- D: Three minutes

That call will cost you no more than

- A: One pound
- B: Fifty pence
- C: Seven euros
- D: Two pounds

How long are the shortlisted contestants given to answer the 'nearest to' question?

- A: One minute
- B: Ten minutes
- C: Thirty seconds
- D: Twenty seconds

A maximum of how many 'phone friends' are contestants allowed to have?

- A: Five
- B: Ten
- C: Fifteen
- D: One

To participate in *Millionaire* you must

- A: Have blonde hair and long legs
- B: Be British
- C: Never have participated before
- D: Be 16 or over

Once in the hot-seat how many questions do you have to answer correctly to win £1,000,000?

- A: A million
- B: Fifty
- C: Fifteen
- D: Twenty-one

Whose signature is on the cheques that winners can actually bank?

- ◆ A: Chris Tarrant's
- ◆ B: Paul Smith's
- ◆ C: David Liddiment's
- ◆ D: Mickey Mouse's

Approximately how many phone lines are there to handle the 09002 44 44 44* calls?

- ◆ A: Five
- ◆ B: Fifty
- ◆ C: Five hundred
- ◆ D: Five thousand

If you're a contestant on the show, what solid colour are you advised not to wear?

- ◆ A: Red
- ◆ B: Blue
- ◆ C: White
- ◆ D: Black

What's the fastest-ever Fastest Finger First?

- ◆ A: One second
- ◆ B: 5.3 seconds
- ◆ C: 3.5 seconds
- ◆ D: 2.1 seconds

How much — to the nearest penny — of each pound generated from phone calls goes towards the prizes?

* A: 48p
* B: 1p
* C: 99p
* D: 69p

How much money from the phone calls goes to production company Celador and its shareholders?

* A: A half
* B: A third
* C: A quarter
* D: None

So where does the rest of the money go?

* A: Not telling
* B: To an offshore trust
* C: To ITV
* D: Other

ANSWERS ON PAGE 128

Answers

09002 44 44 44 Questions: 1. B: Cooper; 2. D: Argentina; 3. A: A guitar; 4. D: Horse chestnuts.

The Shortlist: examples of "Nearest to" questions: 1. 528 (8 minutes, 47.8 seconds); 2. 4626; 3. 25,143.

Put Yourself in The Hot-Seat!: £100, A: Carol; £200, B: Fawn; £300, D: Leo; £500, A: Davy Jones;
£1,000, B: Halloween; £2,000, D: Plimsoll Line; £4,000, B: Silver; £8,000, B: Black Rod; £16,000, B: Royal Flush;
£32,000, B: Diode (Light Emitting Diode); £64,000, C: Volvo; £125,000, B: Sir Bedivere;
£250,000, C: Gibraltar; £500,000, A: Pennsylvania; £1,000,000, D: Neptune.

Questions That Tripped Them Up: 1. A: America; 2. C: The Lancet – 1823; 3. C: Friendship7; 4. B: Librarian.

Are You Sure? Test yourself on your favourite show: 1. B: Two minutes; 2. A: One pound; 3. D: Twenty seconds;
4. A: Five; 5. D: Be 16 or over; 6. C: Fifteen; 7. A: Chris Tarrant's; 8. D: Five thousand; 9. D: Black; 10. D: 2.1 seconds;
11. A: 48p; 12. D: None; 13. D: Other; the rest of the money goes to the telecommunications operator and the
service providers (of the phone lines) and costs specifically related to the publicity and contestant
selection and of course the government (V.A.T.)

* Calls cost 50p per minute and last no longer than 2 minutes.

Everyone at Who Wants To Be A Millionaire? would like to thank the following for making the show such a success:

Stephen Adnitt, Andy Agar, Steve Allen, Cherry Alston, Sven Arnstein, Sarah Ashmore, Barclays Bank, Jo Barker, Sarah Barker, Eleanor Belfrage, Adam Berger, David Bergg, Liz Berry, Chris Bluett, Jim Boyers, Bradstock Insurance Brokers, David Briggs, Broadsystem, Nick Bryce-Smith, Pippa Burridge, Sam Carter, Christian Cerisola, Susie Charrington, Andrew Chichon, Jeanette Childs, Don Christopher, Paul Clark, Pascal Contos, Creative Technology, Duncan Cross, Steve Culshaw, Howard Daimant, Phil Davies, Mat Denton, Kevin Duff, Richard Easter, Jenny Eden, Richard Ellis, Fiona Else, Elstree Film Studios, Griff Evans, Tony Everden, Richard Eyre, Mathew Firsht, Jane Fletcher, Susie Foley, Sophie Forsyth, Fountain Television, James Fox, Sue Fox, Guy Freeman, Sheri French, Freud Communications, Mathew Freud, John Fyfe, Gaebel Watkins & Taylor Ltd, Stuart Gain, John Galbraith, Chris Goss, Phil Grace, Alex Green, Sam Hall, Catriona Halsby, Julia Hancock, Gavin Handman, John Hardie, Anna Heighway, Tim Highmoor, Jaine Hilston, Suzanne Hitchings, Claire Hopkins, Keith Hunter, Colman Hutchinson, ITV Network Ltd, Mark Jay, Simon Johnson, Alex Johnston, Jump, Amanda Kean, Patrick Keegan, Billy Kimberley, Maria Knibbs, Steve Knight, Julian Kossick, KPMG, David Liddiment, Hannah Lillie, Phil Lofthouse, Michael Longmire, Darren Lovell, Simon Lucas, Jason Lunn, Russell Mann, June Mason, Lisle Middleditch, Carol Millward, Barry Mizen, Jadie Montgomery, Patricia Mordecai, Amanda Morris, Chloe Murray, Steve Murray, Naomi Neufeld, Mark Ninnim, Richard Norley, O'Connor Design Consultants, Chris O'Connor, Jason O'Sullivan, Mike Osborne, Richard Park, Steve Parker, Mike Paterson, Brian Pearce, Jerry Peck, Powerhouse, Irena Procyk, David Prosser, Ali Ratcliffe, Neville Reid, Caroline Reik, Ian Reith, Paul Richmond, Brian Ritchie, Claudia Rosencrantz, Jane Rudland, Alice Sagar-Musgrave, Mark Sangster, Siobhan Schafer, Martin Scott, Sarah Sherwin, Peter Simon, Jackie Skilton, Chrissy Smith, Ollie Smith, Richard Standing, Ryan Stephenson, Richard Stevenson, Roz Storey, Keith Strachan, Mathew Strachan, Chris Tarrant, The Edit Works, Chris Thorpe, Kris Thykier, Rob Townsend, Ray Turner, Vari-lite Europe Ltd, Mike Vaughan, Rob Wahl, Andy Walmsley, Elly Warner, Ellis Watson, Keith Watts, Tom Welsh, Mike Whitehill, Julie Wicks, Susan Willer, Jude Winstanley, Helen Wood, Adrian Woolfe, Charles Yates, David Yelland.